THE VICTOR'S TOPICAL BIBLE

Defeating Stress, Depression, and Burnout

By:
Bishop Ronnie Shaw, PhD

The **Victor's** **Topical** **Bible:** *Defeating Stress, Depression, and Burnout* by: Bishop Ronnie Shaw, PhD

Published by Ronnie Shaw Ministries

All Scripture references are from the King James Version of the Holy Bible.

Cover design by Patricia Hilton

ISBN 978-0-9768749-5-9

Contents

Message from the Bishop i

1. Accomplishments...1

2. Anxiety/Worry 5

3. Attitude 9

4. Balance 13

5. Blessings 17

6. Boundaries 23

7. Children 25

8. Compassion 29

9. Counsel 33

10. Courage 39

11. Criticism 43

12. Debt 47

13. Depression 51

14. Discipline 55

15. Education/Knowledge 57

16. Ego/Pride 63

17. Encouragement 71

18. Fear 77

19. Fidelity/Faithfulness................................85

20. Forgiveness 89

21. Frustration 95

22. Habits 99

23. Health 105

24. Honesty 109

25. Hope 115

26. Joy 121

27. Laughter 127

28. Loyalty 131

29. Marriage 135

30. Money/Wealth 141

31. Obedience 149

32. The Past 157

33. Peace 161

34. Planning/Goals 169

35. Prayer 173

36. Rest 177

37. Self-Control 183

38. Self-Examination 187

39. Speech 191

40. Spirituality 197

41. Strength 203

42. Stress 209

43. Submission 213

44. Success 217

45. Thought Life 221

46. Time Management 225

47. Tithing 229

48. Victory 233

49. Work 237

50. Worship 241

MESSAGE FROM THE BISHOP

Stress, depression, and burnout, are real. They destroy individuals, families, and careers. Most people recognize the onset of this motley crew, but have no idea how to address or defeat them.

Sometimes the best gift we can receive during our crises is an encouraging word. The greatest source of encouragement is the Word of God. The Word has the ability to break whatever may bind us. It is the hammer, that will break the hardened areas of our lives (Je. 23:29) and the sword that can divide and discern soulish desires from those of the spirit (He. 4:12).

The Lord sent His Word to heal the brokenhearted and set free those who are bound (Ps. 107:20; Lk. 4:18). Because we face stress, does not mean we need to allow it to overtake us.

God destined us to win. We should not give stress, depression, and burnout the ability to rule another day in our lives.

1

ACCOMPLISHMENTS

One of the last things anyone wants is to come to the end of his or her life and lie on their deathbed thinking, *"I wish I would have. . ."* However, attempting to do more than you are "wired" to do is a prescription for stress and burnout.

1 Samuel 26:25

Then Saul said to David, Blessed be thou, my son David: thou shalt both do great things, and also shalt still prevail. So David went on his way, and Saul returned to his place.

Proverbs 12:3

A man shall not be established by wickedness: but the root of the righteous shall not be moved.

Ecclesiastes 1:1-8

The words of the Preacher, the son of David, king in Jerusalem.

Vanity of vanities, saith the Preacher, vanity of vanities; all is vanity.

What profit hath a man of all his labour which he taketh under the sun?

One generation passeth away, and another generation cometh: but the earth abideth for ever.

The sun also ariseth, and the sun goeth down, and hasteth to his place where he arose.

The wind goeth toward the south, and turneth about unto the north; it whirleth about continually, and the wind returneth again according to his circuits.

All the rivers run into the sea; yet the sea is not full; unto the place from whence the rivers come, thither they return again.

All things are full of labour; man cannot utter it: the eye is not satisfied with seeing, nor the ear filled with hearing.

Daniel 11:24

He shall enter peaceably even upon the fattest places of the province; and he shall do that which his fathers have not done, nor his fathers' fathers; he shall scatter among them the prey, and spoil, and riches: yea, and he shall forecast his devices against the strong holds, even for a time.

Luke 14:28-30

For which of you, intending to build a tower, sitteth not down first, and counteth the cost, whether he have sufficient to finish it?

Lest haply, after he hath laid the foundation, and is not able to finish it, all that behold it begin to mock him,

Saying, This man began to build, and was not able to finish.

1 Peter 2:9-10

But ye are a chosen generation, a royal priesthood, an holy nation, a peculiar people; that ye should shew forth the praises of him who hath called you out of darkness into his marvellous light:

Which in time past were not a people, but are now the people of God: which had not obtained mercy, but now have obtained mercy.

2

ANXIETY/WORRY

Anxiety/worry is probably the most unproductive of our emotions/actions. If we can change the situation that is causing the worry, we should change it rather than worry. If we cannot change it, worrying will not make it better. Ceasing from anxiety/worry begins with a decision. The only thing anxiety/worry will do is intensify the stress levels and deepen any depression. Stop worrying and lessen the stress.

Psalms 37:5

Commit thy way unto the LORD; trust also in him; and he shall bring it to pass.

Psalms 39:6

Surely every man walketh in a vain shew: surely they are disquieted in vain: he heapeth up riches, and knoweth not who shall gather them.

Psalms 55:22

Cast thy burden upon the LORD, and he shall sustain thee: he shall never suffer the righteous to be moved.

Psalms 127:2

It is vain for you to rise up early, to sit up late, to eat the bread of sorrows: for so he giveth his beloved sleep.

Proverbs 15:16

Better is little with the fear of the LORD than great treasure and trouble therewith.

Proverbs 16:3

Commit thy works unto the LORD, and thy thoughts shall be established.

Jeremiah 17:7-8

Blessed is the man that trusteth in the LORD, and whose hope the LORD is.

For he shall be as a tree planted by the waters, and that spreadeth out her roots by the river, and shall not see when heat cometh, but her leaf shall be green; and shall not be careful in the year of drought, neither shall cease from yielding fruit.

Matthew 6:31-34

Therefore take no thought, saying, What shall we eat? or, What shall we drink? or, Wherewithal shall we be clothed?

(For after all these things do the Gentiles seek:) for your heavenly Father knoweth that ye have need of all these things.

But seek ye first the kingdom of God, and his righteousness; and all these things shall be added unto you.

Take therefore no thought for the morrow: for the morrow shall take thought for the things of itself. Sufficient unto the day is the evil thereof.

Luke 12:22-24

And he said unto his disciples, Therefore I say unto you, Take no thought for your life, what ye shall eat; neither for the body, what ye shall put on.

The life is more than meat, and the body is more than raiment.

Consider the ravens: for they neither sow nor reap; which neither have storehouse nor barn; and God feedeth them: how much more are ye better than the fowls?

Philippians 4:6-7

Be careful for nothing; but in every thing by prayer and supplication with thanksgiving let your requests be made known unto God.

And the peace of God, which passeth all understanding, shall keep your hearts and minds through Christ Jesus.

1 Peter 5:7

Casting all your care upon him; for he careth for you.

3

ATTITUDE

Our attitude determines how high we advance in life. People can survive or accomplish almost anything if they have the right attitude. A wrong attitude is an invitation to stress and burnout.

Exodus 14:13-14

And Moses said unto the people, Fear ye not, stand still, and see the salvation of the Lord, which he will shew to you to day: for the Egyptians whom ye have seen to day, ye shall see them again no more for ever.

The Lord shall fight for you, and ye shall hold your peace.

Ruth 2:7

And she said, I pray you, let me glean and gather after the reapers among the sheaves: so she came, and hath continued even from the morning until now, that she tarried a little in the house.

Proverbs 29:25

The fear of man bringeth a snare: but whoso putteth his trust in the Lord shall be safe.

Matthew 5:44-45

But I say unto you, Love your enemies, bless them that curse you, do good to them that hate you, and pray for them which despitefully use you, and persecute you;

That ye may be the children of your Father which is in heaven: for he maketh his sun to rise on the evil and on the good, and sendeth rain on the just and on the unjust.

Philippians 2:1-4

If there be therefore any consolation in Christ, if any comfort of love, if any fellowship of the Spirit, if any bowels and mercies,

Fulfil ye my joy, that ye be likeminded, having the same love, being of one accord, of one mind.

Let nothing be done through strife or vainglory; but in lowliness of mind let each esteem other better than themselves.

Look not every man on his own things, but every man also on the things of others.

Philippians 4:6-7

Be careful for nothing; but in every thing by prayer and supplication with thanksgiving let your requests be made known unto God.

And the peace of God, which passeth all understanding, shall keep your hearts and minds through Christ Jesus.

Philippians 4:13

I can do all things through Christ which strengtheneth me.

1 John 2:15-16

Love not the world, neither the things that are in the world. If any man love the world, the love of the Father is not in him.

For all that is in the world, the lust of the flesh, and the lust of the eyes, and the pride of life, is not of the Father, but is of the world.

4

BALANCE

Everything God created, He created in balance. For north, there is south. For east, there is west. For day, there is night. For the North Pole, there is the South Pole. Things out of balance end in destruction. Keeping our lives in balance greatly aids in a life free from stress, depression, and burnout.

Psalms 57:7

My heart is fixed, O God, my heart is fixed: I will sing and give praise.

Psalms 112:7

He shall not be afraid of evil tidings: his heart is fixed, trusting in the Lord.

Proverbs 11:19

As righteousness tendeth to life: so he that pursueth evil pursueth it to his own death.

Isaiah 26:3

Thou wilt keep him in perfect peace, whose mind is stayed on thee: because he trusteth in thee.

1 Corinthians 15:58

Therefore, my beloved brethren, be ye stedfast, unmoveable, always abounding in the work of the Lord, forasmuch as ye know that your labour is not in vain in the Lord.

Colossians 1:11, 23

Strengthened with all might, according to his glorious power, unto all patience and longsuffering with joyfulness. . .

If ye continue in the faith grounded and settled, and be not moved away from the hope of the gospel, which ye have heard, and which was preached to every creature which is under heaven; whereof I Paul am made a minister.

Hebrews 10:23

Let us hold fast the profession of our faith without wavering; (for he is faithful that promised;)

Every blessing
ignored
becomes
a curse.

— Paulo Coelho

5

BLESSINGS

An old hymn of the Church contained a line that exhorted us to *"count your many blessings, name the one by one."* Looking at our blessings rather than our problems is a great weapon against stress, depression, and burnout.

Deuteronomy 15:4

Save when there shall be no poor among you; for the Lord shall greatly bless thee in the land which the Lord thy God giveth thee for an inheritance to possess it.

Deuteronomy 15:6

For the Lord thy God blesseth thee, as he promised thee: and thou shalt lend unto many nations, but thou shalt not borrow; and thou shalt reign over many nations, but they shall not reign over thee.

Joshua 1:8

This book of the law shall not depart out of thy mouth; but thou shalt meditate therein day and night, that thou mayest observe to do according to all that is written therein: for then thou shalt make thy way prosperous, and then thou shalt have good success.

1 Kings 2:3

And keep the charge of the Lord thy God, to walk in his ways, to keep his statutes, and his commandments, and his judgments, and his testimonies, as it is written in the law of Moses, that thou mayest prosper in all that thou doest, and whithersoever thou turnest thyself:

1 Kings 8:23

And he said, Lord God of Israel, there is no God like thee, in heaven above, or on earth beneath, who keepest covenant and mercy with thy servants that walk before thee with all their heart.

Job 36:11

If they obey and serve him, they shall spend their days in prosperity, and their years in pleasures.

Psalms 2:12

Kiss the Son, lest he be angry, and ye perish from the way, when his wrath is kindled but a little. Blessed are all they that put their trust in him.

Psalms 34:1-4

I will bless the Lord at all times: his praise shall continually be in my mouth.

My soul shall make her boast in the Lord: the humble shall hear thereof, and be glad.

O magnify the Lord with me, and let us exalt his name together.

I sought the Lord, and he heard me, and delivered me from all my fears.

Psalms 34:8

O taste and see that the Lord is good: blessed is the man that trusteth in him.

Psalms 40:4

Blessed is that man that maketh the Lord his trust, and respecteth not the proud, nor such as turn aside to lies.

Psalms 68:19

Blessed be the Lord, who daily loadeth us with benefits, even the God of our salvation. Selah.

Psalms 112:1-3

Praise ye the Lord. Blessed is the man that feareth the Lord, that delighteth greatly in his commandments.

His seed shall be mighty upon earth: the generation of the upright shall be blessed.

Wealth and riches shall be in his house: and his righteousness endureth for ever.

Proverbs 16:7

When a man's ways please the Lord, he maketh even his enemies to be at peace with him.

Luke 1:45

And blessed is she that believed: for there shall be a performance of those things which were told her from the Lord.

Galatians 3:9

So then they which be of faith are blessed with faithful Abraham.

Ephesians 1:3-4

Blessed be the God and Father of our Lord Jesus Christ, who hath blessed us with all spiritual blessings in heavenly places in Christ:

According as he hath chosen us in him before the foundation of the world, that we should be holy and without blame before him in love:

James 1:12

Blessed is the man that endureth temptation: for when he is tried, he shall receive the crown of life, which the Lord hath promised to them that love him.

Boundaries are to protect life, not to limit pleasures.

— Edwin Louis Cole

6

BOUNDARIES

Boundaries are a vital part of life. People pay surveyors to define property lines so they may protect their property. Pet owners use fences or electronic devices to keep animals within certain perimeters for the animals' protection as well as reducing liability. A life without boundaries is a life destined for stress.

Deuteronomy 19:14

Thou shalt not remove thy neighbour's landmark, which they of old time have set in thine inheritance, which thou shalt inherit in the land that the Lord thy God giveth thee to possess it.

Deuteronomy 27:17

Cursed be he that removeth his neighbour's landmark. And all the people shall say, Amen.

Job 24:2

Some remove the landmarks; they violently take away flocks, and feed thereof.

Psalms 139:5

Thou hast beset me behind and before, and laid thine hand upon me.

Proverbs 22:28

Remove not the ancient landmark, which thy fathers have set.

Proverbs 23:10

Remove not the old landmark; and enter not into the fields of the fatherless.

Hosea 5:10

The princes of Judah were like them that remove the bound: therefore I will pour out my wrath upon them like water.

7

CHILDREN

Children are a blessing from God. A hundred years from now it will not matter what type of car we drove, what type of house we lived in, or the size of our bank account. What will matter is what we sowed into the life of a child. Stress, depression, and burnout, directly and unfairly affect our children.

Genesis 17:7-8

And I will establish my covenant between me and thee and thy seed after thee in their generations for an everlasting covenant, to be a God unto thee, and to thy seed after thee.

And I will give unto thee, and to thy seed after thee, the land wherein thou art a stranger, all the land of Canaan, for an everlasting possession; and I will be their God.

Exodus 34:7

Keeping mercy for thousands, forgiving iniquity and transgression and sin, and that will by no means clear the guilty; visiting the iniquity of the fathers upon the children, and upon the children's children, unto the third and to the fourth generation.

Psalms 127:3-5

Lo, children are an heritage of the Lord: and the fruit of the womb is his reward.

As arrows are in the hand of a mighty man; so are children of the youth.

Happy is the man that hath his quiver full of them: they shall not be ashamed, but they shall speak with the enemies in the gate.

Psalms 128:3

Thy wife shall be as a fruitful vine by the sides of thine house: thy children like olive plants round about thy table.

Matthew 19:14

But Jesus said, Suffer little children, and forbid them not, to come unto me: for of such is the kingdom of heaven.

1 Corinthians 7:14

For the unbelieving husband is sanctified by the wife, and the unbelieving wife is sanctified by the husband: else were your children unclean; but now are they holy.

Ephesians 6:1-4

Children, obey your parents in the Lord: for this is right.

Honour thy father and mother; (which is the first commandment with promise;)

That it may be well with thee, and thou mayest live long on the earth.

And, ye fathers, provoke not your children to wrath: but bring them up in the nurture and admonition of the Lord.

8

COMPASSION

There are many benefits to living a compassionate lifestyle. According to a National Institute of Health study, compassion makes people happier and more attractive that non-compassionate people. Compassion boosts our health and longevity, and has the ability to pull us out of *"the funk."* Stress and depression are *"funk,"* and anything that can pull us out of it is worthwhile.

Deuteronomy 10:18-19

He doth execute the judgment of the fatherless and widow, and loveth the stranger, in giving him food and raiment.

Love ye therefore the stranger: for ye were strangers in the land of Egypt.

Job 6:14

To him that is afflicted pity should be shewed from his friend; but he forsaketh the fear of the Almighty.

Psalms 35:12-14

They rewarded me evil for good to the spoiling of my soul.

But as for me, when they were sick, my clothing was sackcloth: I humbled my soul with fasting; and my prayer returned into mine own bosom.

I behaved myself as though he had been my friend or brother: I bowed down heavily, as one that mourneth for his mother.

Proverbs 19:17

He that hath pity upon the poor lendeth unto the Lord; and that which he hath given will he pay him again.

Romans 12:15

Rejoice with them that do rejoice, and weep with them that weep.

1 Corinthians 9:22

To the weak became I as weak, that I might gain the weak: I am made all things to all men, that I might by all means save some.

1 Corinthians 12:25-26

That there should be no schism in the body; but that the members should have the same care one for another.

And whether one member suffer, all the members suffer with it; or one member be honoured, all the members rejoice with it.

Galatians 6:2

Bear ye one another's burdens, and so fulfil the law of Christ.

1 Peter 3:8

Finally, be ye all of one mind, having compassion one of another, love as brethren, be pitiful, be courteous.

1 John 3:17

But whoso hath this world's good, and seeth his brother have need, and shutteth up his bowels of compassion from him, how dwelleth the love of God in him?

9

COUNSEL

We should honor, those who love us enough to tell us what we need to hear, rather than those who tell us what we want to hear. Sometimes God speaks to us through the wise counsel of others. Accepting wise counsel greatly reduces our chances of stress, depression, and burnout.

Numbers 14:6-10

And Joshua the son of Nun, and Caleb the son of Jephunneh, which were of them that searched the land, rent their clothes:

And they spake unto all the company of the children of Israel, saying, The land, which we passed through to search it, is an exceeding good land.

If the Lord delight in us, then he will bring us into this land, and give it us; a land which floweth with milk and honey.

Only rebel not ye against the Lord, neither fear ye the people of the land; for they are bread for us: their defence is departed from them, and the Lord is with us: fear them not.

But all the congregation bade stone them with stones. And the glory of the Lord appeared in the tabernacle of the congregation before all the children of Israel.

Psalms 33:11

The counsel of the Lord standeth for ever, the thoughts of his heart to all generations.

Proverbs 1:5-6

A wise man will hear, and will increase learning; and a man of understanding shall attain unto wise counsels:

To understand a proverb, and the interpretation; the words of the wise, and their dark sayings.

Proverbs 1:24-26

Because I have called, and ye refused; I have stretched out my hand, and no man regarded;

But ye have set at nought all my counsel, and would none of my reproof:

I also will laugh at your calamity; I will mock when your fear cometh;

Proverbs 9:9

Give instruction to a wise man, and he will be yet wiser: teach a just man, and he will increase in learning.

Proverbs 11:14

Where no counsel is, the people fall: but in the multitude of counsellors there is safety.

Proverbs 12:15

The way of a fool is right in his own eyes: but he that hearkeneth unto counsel is wise.

Proverbs 15:22

Without counsel purposes are disappointed: but in the multitude of counsellors they are established.

Proverbs 19:20-21

Hear counsel, and receive instruction, that thou mayest be wise in thy latter end.

There are many devices in a man's heart; nevertheless the counsel of the Lord, that shall stand.

Proverbs 20:18

Every purpose is established by counsel: and with good advice make war.

Proverbs 24:6

For by wise counsel thou shalt make thy war: and in multitude of counsellors there is safety.

Proverbs 27:5-6

Open rebuke is better than secret love.

Faithful are the wounds of a friend; but the kisses of an enemy are deceitful.

Proverbs 27:9

Ointment and perfume rejoice the heart: so doth the sweetness of a man's friend by hearty counsel.

Isaiah 1:26

And I will restore thy judges as at the first, and thy counsellors as at the beginning: afterward thou shalt be called, The city of righteousness, the faithful city

Luke 14:31

Or what king, going to make war against another king, sitteth not down first, and consulteth whether he be able with ten thousand to meet him that cometh against him with twenty thousand?

Courage is being scared to death... and saddling up anyway.

— John Wayne

10

COURAGE

Courage – everyone wants it, but not everyone has it or exemplifies it. There are instances of amazing courage displayed, from Scripture, to Hollywood movies. Often we could minimize our stress and burnout if we would display some courage.

Deuteronomy 31:6

Be strong and of a good courage, fear not, nor be afraid of them: for the Lord thy God, he it is that doth go with thee; he will not fail thee, nor forsake thee.

Deuteronomy 31:8

And the Lord, he it is that doth go before thee; he will be with thee, he will not fail thee, neither forsake thee: fear not, neither be dismayed.

Deuteronomy 33:27

The eternal God is thy refuge, and underneath are the everlasting arms: and he shall thrust out the enemy from before thee; and shall say, Destroy them.

Joshua 10:25

And Joshua said unto them, Fear not, nor be dismayed, be strong and of good courage: for thus shall the Lord do to all your enemies against whom ye fight.

Ezra 10:4

Arise; for this matter belongeth unto thee: we also will be with thee: be of good courage, and do it.

Psalms 18:30

As for God, his way is perfect: the word of the Lord is tried: he is a buckler to all those that trust in him.

Proverbs 28:1

The wicked flee when no man pursueth: but the righteous are bold as a lion.

1 Corinthians 16:13

Watch ye, stand fast in the faith, quit you like men, be strong.

Philippians 1:27-28

Only let your conversation be as it becometh the gospel of Christ: that whether I come and see you, or else be absent, I may hear of your affairs, that ye stand fast in one spirit, with one mind striving together for the faith of the gospel;

And in nothing terrified by your adversaries: which is to them an evident token of perdition, but to you of salvation, and that of God.

I like criticism. It makes you strong.

— LeBron James

11

CRITICISM

Many have trouble receiving criticism, even when it is constructive in nature. However, we do not seem to have trouble criticizing others. We should not allow criticism to become a source of offence in our lives, because of the amount of stress and depression it can inflict. Regardless of how criticism is given, receive it as a blessing and move on. It is better for one person to criticize us, and we address the issue, than to ignore it and become the laughingstock of hundreds.

Psalms 141:5

Let the righteous smite me; it shall be a kindness: and let him reprove me; it shall be an excellent oil, which shall not break my head: for yet my prayer also shall be in their calamities.

Proverbs 9:7-9

He that reproveth a scorner getteth to himself shame: and he that rebuketh a wicked man getteth himself a blot.

Reprove not a scorner, lest he hate thee: rebuke a wise man, and he will love thee.

Give instruction to a wise man, and he will be yet wiser: teach a just man, and he will increase in learning.

Proverbs 27:5-6

Open rebuke is better than secret love.

Faithful are the wounds of a friend; but the kisses of an enemy are deceitful.

Matthew 7:1-5

Judge not, that ye be not judged.

For with what judgment ye judge, ye shall be judged: and with what measure ye mete, it shall be measured to you again.

And why beholdest thou the mote that is in thy brother's eye, but considerest not the beam that is in thine own eye?

Or how wilt thou say to thy brother, Let me pull out the mote out of thine eye; and, behold, a beam is in thine own eye?

Thou hypocrite, first cast out the beam out of thine own eye; and then shalt thou see clearly to cast out the mote out of thy brother's eye.

John 7:24

Judge not according to the appearance, but judge righteous judgment.

Romans 2:1

Therefore thou art inexcusable, O man, whosoever thou art that judgest: for wherein thou judgest another, thou condemnest thyself; for thou that judgest doest the same things.

Romans 14:13

Let us not therefore judge one another any more: but judge this rather, that no man put a stumblingblock or an occasion to fall in his brother's way.

Galatians 5:15

But if ye bite and devour one another, take heed that ye be not consumed one of another.

James 4:11-12

Speak not evil one of another, brethren. He that speaketh evil of his brother, and judgeth his brother, speaketh evil of the law, and judgeth the law: but if thou judge the law, thou art not a doer of the law, but a judge.

There is one lawgiver, who is able to save and to destroy: who art thou that judgest another?

12

DEBT

Debt is an enslaver. It entices people to buy much of what they do not need, with money they do not have, to impress people they do not know. Debt is a huge contributor to stress and depression. If we are to ease the stress, and its effects on our lives, we must put debt behind us.

1 Samuel 22:2

And every one that was in distress, and every one that was in debt, and every one that was discontented, gathered themselves unto him; and he became a captain over them: and there were with him about four hundred men.

2 Kings 4:1

Now there cried a certain woman of the wives of the sons of the prophets unto Elisha, saying, Thy servant my husband is dead; and thou knowest that thy servant did fear the Lord: and the creditor is come to take unto him my two sons to be bondmen.

2 Kings 4:7

Then she came and told the man of God. And he said, Go, sell the oil, and pay thy debt, and live thou and thy children of the rest.

Nehemiah 5:4-5

There were also that said, We have borrowed money for the king's tribute, and that upon our lands and vineyards.

Yet now our flesh is as the flesh of our brethren, our children as their children: and, lo, we bring into bondage our sons and our daughters to be servants, and some of our daughters are brought unto bondage already: neither is it in our power to redeem them; for other men have our lands and vineyards.

Proverbs 22:7

The rich ruleth over the poor, and the borrower is servant to the lender.

Isaiah 24:2

And it shall be, as with the people, so with the priest; as with the servant, so with his master; as with the maid, so with her mistress; as with the buyer, so with the seller; as with the lender, so with the borrower; as with the taker of usury, so with the giver of usury to him.

Matthew 6:12

And forgive us our debts, as we forgive our debtors.

Romans 1:14

I am debtor both to the Greeks, and to the Barbarians; both to the wise, and to the unwise.

Romans 13:7-8

Render therefore to all their dues: tribute to whom tribute is due; custom to whom custom; fear to whom fear; honour to whom honour.

Owe no man any thing, but to love one another: for he that loveth another hath fulfilled the law.

13

DEPRESSION

Clinical depression is wicked. It can make an extrovert think like an introvert overnight. It can drain every ounce of joy and leave the individual in a cloud of hopelessness and despair. Depression not dealt with, quickly can lead to bouts of oppression, further resulting in physical illnesses. Do not give depression a foothold.

Deuteronomy 28:67

In the morning thou shalt say, Would God it were even! and at even thou shalt say, Would God it were morning! for the fear of thine heart wherewith thou shalt fear, and for the sight of thine eyes which thou shalt see.

1 Kings 19:3-4

And when he saw that, he arose, and went for his life, and came to Beersheba, which belongeth to Judah, and left his servant there.

But he himself went a day's journey into the wilderness, and came and sat down under a juniper tree: and he requested for himself that he might die; and said, It is enough; now, O Lord, take away my life; for I am not better than my fathers.

Psalms 42:5-6

Why art thou cast down, O my soul? and why art thou disquieted in me? hope thou in God: for I shall yet praise him for the help of his countenance.

O my God, my soul is cast down within me: therefore will I remember thee from the land of Jordan, and of the Hermonites, from the hill Mizar.

Ecclesiastes 2:20

Therefore I went about to cause my heart to despair of all the labour which I took under the sun.

2 Corinthians 4:8-12

We are troubled on every side, yet not distressed; we are perplexed, but not in despair;

Persecuted, but not forsaken; cast down, but not destroyed;

Always bearing about in the body the dying of the Lord Jesus, that the life also of Jesus might be made manifest in our body.

For we which live are alway delivered unto death for Jesus' sake, that the life also of Jesus might be made manifest in our mortal flesh.

So then death worketh in us, but life in you.

2 Corinthians 10:3-4

For though we walk in the flesh, we do not war after the flesh:

(For the weapons of our warfare are not carnal, but mighty through God to the pulling down of strong holds;).

Philippians 4:6

Be careful for nothing; but in every thing by prayer and supplication with thanksgiving let your requests be made known unto God.

14

DISCIPLINE

Jim Rohn said, *"Everyone must choose one of two pains: The pain of discipline or the pain of regret."* A life without discipline is a life destined for destruction. God wants us to live our lives in such a state of discipline/self-control, that He made it a fruit of His Spirit. If we live our lives with discipline, we have less chance of being a victim of stress, depression, or burnout.

Proverbs 16:32

He that is slow to anger is better than the mighty; and he that ruleth his spirit than he that taketh a city.

Proverbs 25:28

He that hath no rule over his own spirit is like a city that is broken down, and without walls.

Proverbs 29:11

A fool uttereth all his mind: but a wise man keepeth it in till afterwards.

1 Corinthians 7:5

Defraud ye not one the other, except it be with consent for a time, that ye may give yourselves to fasting and prayer; and come together again, that Satan tempt you not for your incontinency.

1 Corinthians 9:25

And every man that striveth for the mastery is temperate in all things. Now they do it to obtain a corruptible crown; but we an incorruptible.

Galatians 5:22-23

But the fruit of the Spirit is love, joy, peace, longsuffering, gentleness, goodness, faith,

Meekness, temperance: against such there is no law.

15

EDUCATION/KNOWLEDGE

What one does not know can be very dangerous. Someone that knows the cause of his or her physical ailment can get medicine to fix the problem. Someone that knows of a financial "sure thing" can secure a financial future overnight. When we properly educate ourselves, it decreases our possibility of stress, depression, and burnout victimization.

Psalms 78:5-7

For he established a testimony in Jacob, and appointed a law in Israel, which he commanded our fathers, that they should make them known to heir children:

That the generation to come might know them, even the children which should be born; who should arise and declare them to their children:

That they might set their hope in God, and not forget the works of God, but keep his commandments.

Psalms 119:66

Teach me good judgment and knowledge: for I have believed thy commandments.

Proverbs 1:1-5

The proverbs of Solomon the son of David, king of Israel;

To know wisdom and instruction; to perceive the words of understanding;

To receive the instruction of wisdom, justice, and judgment, and equity;

To give subtilty to the simple, to the young man knowledge and discretion.

A wise man will hear, and will increase learning; and a man of understanding shall attain unto wise counsels.

Proverbs 2:1-5

My son, if thou wilt receive my words, and hide my commandments with thee;

So that thou incline thine ear unto wisdom, and apply thine heart to understanding;

Yea, if thou criest after knowledge, and liftest up thy voice for understanding;

If thou seekest her as silver, and searchest for her as for hid treasures;

Then shalt thou understand the fear of the Lord, and find the knowledge of God.

Proverbs 10:14

Wise men lay up knowledge: but the mouth of the foolish is near destruction.

Proverbs 12:1

Whoso loveth instruction loveth knowledge: but he that hateth reproof is brutish.

Proverbs 15:14

The heart of him that hath understanding seeketh knowledge: but the mouth of fools feedeth on foolishness.

Proverbs 18:15

The heart of the prudent getteth knowledge; and the ear of the wise seeketh knowledge.

Isaiah 5:13

Therefore my people are gone into captivity, because they have no knowledge: and their honourable men are famished, and their multitude dried up with thirst.

Jeremiah 10:14

Every man is brutish in his knowledge: every founder is confounded by the graven image: for his molten image is falsehood, and there is no breath in them.

Hosea 4:6

My people are destroyed for lack of knowledge: because thou hast rejected knowledge, I will also reject thee, that thou shalt be no priest to me: seeing thou hast forgotten the law of thy God, I will also forget thy children.

Romans 10:2

For I bear them record that they have a zeal of God, but not according to knowledge.

Ephesians 5:17

Wherefore be ye not unwise, but understanding what the will of the Lord is.

Colossians 1:9-10

For this cause we also, since the day we heard it, do not cease to pray for you, and to desire that ye might be filled with the knowledge of his will in all wisdom and spiritual understanding.

That ye might walk worthy of the Lord unto all pleasing, being fruitful in every good work, and increasing in the knowledge of God.

James 3:13

Who is a wise man and endued with knowledge among you? let him shew out of a good conversation his works with meekness of wisdom.

It was pride
that changed
angels into
devils...

— Saint Augustine

16

EGO/PRIDE

There is a big difference between ego and self-esteem. Self-esteem is valuable to the life of an individual. Unfortunately, egos are destructive to us, and to those with whom we connect. An over-inflated ego results in added stress to those whom we allow in our circles.

1 Samuel 15:26-30

And Samuel said unto Saul, I will not return with thee: for thou hast rejected the word of the Lord, and the Lord hath rejected thee from being king over Israel.

And as Samuel turned about to go away, he laid hold upon the skirt of his mantle, and it rent.

And Samuel said unto him, The Lord hath rent the kingdom of Israel from thee this day, and hath given it to a neighbour of thine, that is better than thou.

And also the Strength of Israel will not lie nor repent: for he is not a man, that he should repent.

Then he said, I have sinned: yet honour me now, I pray thee, before the elders of my people, and before Israel, and turn again with me, that I may worship the Lord thy God.

2 Samuel 24:10-15

And David's heart smote him after that he had numbered the people. And David said unto the Lord, I have sinned greatly in that I have done: and now, I beseech thee, O Lord, take away the iniquity of thy servant; for I have done very foolishly.

For when David was up in the morning, the word of the Lord came unto the prophet Gad, David's seer, saying,

Go and say unto David, Thus saith the Lord, I offer thee three things; choose thee one of them, that I may do it unto thee.

So Gad came to David, and told him, and said unto him, Shall seven years of famine come unto thee in thy land? or wilt thou flee three months before thine enemies, while they pursue thee? or that there be three days' pestilence in thy land? now advise, and see what answer I shall return to him that sent me.

And David said unto Gad, I am in a great strait: let us fall now into the hand of the Lord; for his mercies are great: and let me not fall into the hand of man.

So the Lord sent a pestilence upon Israel from the morning even to the time appointed: and there died of the people from Dan even to Beersheba seventy thousand men.

Proverbs 6:16-17

These six things doth the LORD hate: yea, seven are an abomination unto him:

A proud look, a lying tongue, and hands that shed innocent blood.

Proverbs 11:2

When pride cometh, then cometh shame: but with the lowly is wisdom.

Proverbs 13:10

Only by pride cometh contention: but with the well advised is wisdom.

Proverbs 16:5

Every one that is proud in heart is an abomination to the LORD: though hand join in hand, he shall not be unpunished.

Proverbs 16:18

Pride goeth before destruction, and an haughty spirit before a fall.

Proverbs 21:4

An high look, and a proud heart, and the plowing of the wicked, is sin.

Matthew 20:26-27

But it shall not be so among you: but whosoever will be great among you, let him be your minister;

And whosoever will be chief among you, let him be your servant.

Romans 12:1-3

I beseech you therefore, brethren, by the mercies of God, that ye present your bodies a living sacrifice, holy, acceptable unto God, which is your reasonable service.

And be not conformed to this world: but be ye transformed by the renewing of your mind, that ye may prove what is that good, and acceptable, and perfect, will of God.

For I say, through the grace given unto me, to every man that is among you, not to think of himself more highly than he ought to think; but to think soberly, according as God hath dealt to every man the measure of faith.

1 Corinthians 5:6

Your glorying is not good. Know ye not that a little leaven leaveneth the whole lump?

1 Thessalonians 5:11-14

Wherefore comfort yourselves together, and edify one another, even as also ye do.

And we beseech you, brethren, to know them which labour among you, and are over you in the Lord, and admonish you;

And to esteem them very highly in love for their work's sake. And be at peace among yourselves.

Now we exhort you, brethren, warn them that are unruly, comfort the feebleminded, support the weak, be patient toward all men.

1 Timothy 3:5-6

(For if a man know not how to rule his own house, how shall he take care of the church of God?)

Not a novice, lest being lifted up with pride he fall into the condemnation of the devil.

James 4:6

But he giveth more grace. Wherefore he saith, God resisteth the proud, but giveth grace unto the humble.

1 John 2:16

For all that is in the world, the lust of the flesh, and the lust of the eyes, and the pride of life, is not of the Father, but is of the world.

We live by
encouragement
and die without
it - slowly,
sadly and
angrily.

— Celeste Holm

17

ENCOURAGEMENT

Everyone has inner greatness. For most of us to access that greatness, we need encouragement. Receiving encouragement greatly reduces stress, and aids in the lifting of depression and recovery from burnout.

Psalms 119:50

This is my comfort in my affliction: for thy word hath quickened me.

Proverbs 12:25

Heaviness in the heart of man maketh it stoop: but a good word maketh it glad.

Proverbs 15:23

A man hath joy by the answer of his mouth: and a word spoken in due season, how good is it!

Proverbs 25:11

A word fitly spoken is like apples of gold in pictures of silver.

Matthew 25:21

His lord said unto him, Well done, thou good and faithful servant: thou hast been faithful over a few things, I will make thee ruler over many things: enter thou into the joy of thy lord.

2 Corinthians 1:3-4

Blessed be God, even the Father of our Lord Jesus Christ, the Father of mercies, and the God of all comfort;

Who comforteth us in all our tribulation, that we may be able to comfort them which are in any trouble, by the comfort wherewith we ourselves are comforted of God.

Philippians 2:25-30

Yet I supposed it necessary to send to you Epaphroditus, my brother, and companion in labour, and fellowsoldier, but your messenger, and he that ministered to my wants.

For he longed after you all, and was full of heaviness, because that ye had heard that he had been sick.

For indeed he was sick nigh unto death: but God had mercy on him; and not on him only, but on me also, lest I should have sorrow upon sorrow.

I sent him therefore the more carefully, that, when ye see him again, ye may rejoice, and that I may be the less sorrowful.

Receive him therefore in the Lord with all gladness; and hold such in reputation:

Because for the work of Christ he was nigh unto death, not regarding his life, to supply your lack of service toward me.

Philippians 4:13

I can do all things through Christ which strengtheneth me.

Colossians 2:2

That their hearts might be comforted, being knit together in love, and unto all riches of the full assurance of understanding, to the acknowledgement of the mystery of God, and of the Father, and of Christ.

1 Thessalonians 5:11

Wherefore comfort yourselves together, and edify one another, even as also ye do.

Hebrews 3:13

But exhort one another daily, while it is called To day; lest any of you be hardened through the deceitfulness of sin.

Hebrews 12:1-3

Wherefore seeing we also are compassed about with so great a cloud of witnesses, let us lay aside every weight, and the sin which doth so easily beset us, and let us run with patience the race that is set before us,

Looking unto Jesus the author and finisher of our faith; who for the joy that was set before him endured the cross, despising the shame, and is set down at the right hand of the throne of God.

For consider him that endured such contradiction of sinners against himself, lest ye be wearied and faint in your minds.

I'm not afraid of storms, for I'm learning how to sail my ship.

— Louisa May Alcott

18

FEAR

Fear is the absence of faith. Some have declared fear to be the acronym for "False Evidence Appearing Real." Some view it as faith in reverse or the devil's faith. Regardless of how we view it, fear is deadly – i.e. the adage, *"scared to death."* To live free from stress, depression, and burnout, we must remove fear from our lives.

Genesis 15:1

After these things the word of the LORD came unto Abram in a vision, saying, Fear not, Abram: I am thy shield, and thy exceeding great reward.

Genesis 26:24

And the LORD appeared unto him the same night, and said, I am the God of Abraham thy father: fear not, for I am with thee, and will bless thee, and multiply thy seed for my servant Abraham's sake.

Deuteronomy 3:22

Ye shall not fear them: for the LORD your God he shall fight for you.

Deuteronomy 31:6

Be strong and of a good courage, fear not, nor be afraid of them: for the LORD thy God, he it is that doth go with thee; he will not fail thee, nor forsake thee.

Deuteronomy 31:8

And the LORD, he it is that doth go before thee; he will be with thee, he will not fail thee, neither forsake thee: fear not, neither be dismayed.

Joshua 1:9

Have not I commanded thee? Be strong and of a good courage; be not afraid, neither be thou dismayed: for the LORD thy God is with thee whithersoever thou goest.

Psalms 3:5-6

I laid me down and slept; I awaked; for the LORD sustained me.

I will not be afraid of ten thousands of people, that have set themselves against me round about.

Psalms 23:4

Yea, though I walk through the valley of the shadow of death, I will fear no evil: for thou art with me; thy rod and thy staff they comfort me.

Psalms 27:1-3

The LORD is my light and my salvation; whom shall I fear? the LORD is the strength of my life; of whom shall I be afraid?

When the wicked, even mine enemies and my foes, came upon me to eat up my flesh, they stumbled and fell.

Though an host should encamp against me, my heart shall not fear: though war should rise against me, in this will I be confident.

Psalms 34:4

I sought the LORD, and he heard me, and delivered me from all my fears.

Psalms 46:1-3

God is our refuge and strength, a very present help in trouble.

Therefore will not we fear, though the earth be removed, and though the mountains be carried into the midst of the sea;

Though the waters thereof roar and be troubled, though the mountains shake with the swelling thereof. Selah.

Psalms 53:5

There were they in great fear, where no fear was: for God hath scattered the bones of him that encampeth against thee: thou hast put them to shame, because God hath despised them.

Psalms 56:3-4

What time I am afraid, I will trust in thee.

In God I will praise his word, in God I have put my trust; I will not fear what flesh can do unto me.

Psalms 91:5-7

Thou shalt not be afraid for the terror by night; nor for the arrow that flieth by day;

Nor for the pestilence that walketh in darkness; nor for the destruction that wasteth at noonday.

A thousand shall fall at thy side, and ten thousand at thy right hand; but it shall not come nigh thee.

Psalms 112:7

He shall not be afraid of evil tidings: his heart is fixed, trusting in the LORD

Proverbs 3:25-26

Be not afraid of sudden fear, neither of the desolation of the wicked, when it cometh.

For the LORD shall be thy confidence, and shall keep thy foot from being taken.

Isaiah 12:2

Behold, God is my salvation; I will trust, and not be afraid: for the LORD JEHOVAH is my strength and my song; he also is become my salvation.

Isaiah 41:10

Fear thou not; for I am with thee: be not dismayed; for I am thy God: I will strengthen thee; yea, I will help thee; yea, I will uphold thee with the right hand of my righteousness.

Matthew 14:27

But straightway Jesus spake unto them, saying, Be of good cheer; it is I; be not afraid.

Mark 5:36

As soon as Jesus heard the word that was spoken, he saith unto the ruler of the synagogue, Be not afraid, only believe.

2 Timothy 1:7

For God hath not given us the spirit of fear; but of power, and of love, and of a sound mind.

1 John 4:18

There is no fear in love; but perfect love casteth out fear: because fear hath torment. He that feareth is not made perfect in love.

Your faithfulness makes you trustworthy to God.

— Edwin Louis Cole

19

FIDELITY/FAITHFULNESS

Those who practice fidelity, live more satisfying lives than those who do not. The emotional and physical costs of unfaithfulness are higher than the guilty want to pay and the innocent should pay. Infidelity is an offshoot of a stressed, depressed, or burned out life. Get rid of the stress and live a life of faithfulness to God, and others.

Genesis 39:6-8

And he left all that he had in Joseph's hand; and he knew not ought he had, save the bread which he did eat. And Joseph was a goodly person, and well favoured.

And it came to pass after these things, that his master's wife cast her eyes upon Joseph; and she said, Lie with me.

But he refused, and said unto his master's wife, Behold, my master wotteth not what is with me in the house, and he hath committed all that he hath to my hand.

2 Kings 12:15

Moreover they reckoned not with the men, into whose hand they delivered the money to be bestowed on workmen: for they dealt faithfully.

Psalms 31:23

O love the LORD, all ye his saints: for the LORD preserveth the faithful, and plentifully rewardeth the proud doer.

Proverbs 11:13

A talebearer revealeth secrets: but he that is of a faithful spirit concealeth the matter.

Proverbs 20:6

Most men will proclaim every one his own goodness: but a faithful man who can find?

Proverbs 27:6

Faithful are the wounds of a friend; but the kisses of an enemy are deceitful.

Proverbs 28:20

A faithful man shall abound with blessings: but he that maketh haste to be rich shall not be innocent.

Matthew 24:45-47

Who then is a faithful and wise servant, whom his lord hath made ruler over his household, to give them meat in due season?

Blessed is that servant, whom his lord when he cometh shall find so doing.

Verily I say unto you, That he shall make him ruler over all his goods.

Luke 16:10-12

He that is faithful in that which is least is faithful also in much: and he that is unjust in the least is unjust also in much.

If therefore ye have not been faithful in the unrighteous mammon, who will commit to your trust the true riches?

And if ye have not been faithful in that which is another man's, who shall give you that which is your own?

1 Corinthians 4:2

Moreover it is required in stewards, that a man be found faithful.

Revelation 2:10

Fear none of those things which thou shalt suffer: behold, the devil shall cast some of you into prison, that ye may be tried; and ye shall have tribulation ten days: be thou faithful unto death, and I will give thee a crown of life.

20

FORGIVENESS

Often, the chains that shackle us are those, which are self-imposed. They are chains we created by failing to forgive others of wrongs they have done. We can attribute much of our stress and depression to past wrongs that we refuse to turn loose. Forgiveness does not benefit those who have wronged us – it benefits us.

Exodus 23:4-5

If thou meet thine enemy's ox or his ass going astray, thou shalt surely bring it back to him again.

If thou see the ass of him that hateth thee lying under his burden, and wouldest forbear to help him, thou shalt surely help with him.

Proverbs 19:11

The discretion of a man deferreth his anger; and it is his glory to pass over a transgression.

Proverbs 24:17

Rejoice not when thine enemy falleth, and let not thine heart be glad when he stumbleth:

Proverbs 24:29

Say not, I will do so to him as he hath done to me: I will render to the man according to his work.

Proverbs 25:21-22

If thine enemy be hungry, give him bread to eat; and if he be thirsty, give him water to drink:

For thou shalt heap coals of fire upon his head, and the LORD shall reward thee.

Ecclesiastes 7:21-22

Also take no heed unto all words that are spoken; lest thou hear thy servant curse thee:

For oftentimes also thine own heart knoweth that thou thyself likewise hast cursed others.

Matthew 5:7

Blessed are the merciful: for they shall obtain mercy.

Matthew 5:39-41

But I say unto you, That ye resist not evil: but whosoever shall smite thee on thy right cheek, turn to him the other also.

And if any man will sue thee at the law, and take away thy coat, let him have thy cloke also.

And whosoever shall compel thee to go a mile, go with him twain.

Matthew 5:43-44

Ye have heard that it hath been said, Thou shalt love thy neighbour, and hate thine enemy.

But I say unto you, Love your enemies, bless them that curse you, do good to them that hate you, and pray for them which despitefully use you, and persecute you.

Matthew 6:12

And forgive us our debts, as we forgive our debtors.

Matthew 6:14-15

For if ye forgive men their trespasses, your heavenly Father will also forgive you:

But if ye forgive not men their trespasses, neither will your Father forgive your trespasses.

Matthew 18:21-22

Then came Peter to him, and said, Lord, how oft shall my brother sin against me, and I forgive him? till seven times?

Jesus saith unto him, I say not unto thee, Until seven times: but, Until seventy times seven.

Mark 11:25-26

And when ye stand praying, forgive, if ye have ought against any: that your Father also which is in heaven may forgive you your trespasses.

But if ye do not forgive, neither will your Father which is in heaven forgive your trespasses.

Romans 12:14

Bless them which persecute you: bless, and curse not.

Romans 12:17

Recompense to no man evil for evil. Provide things honest in the sight of all men.

Romans 12:19-21

Dearly beloved, avenge not yourselves, but rather give place unto wrath: for it is written, Vengeance is mine; I will repay, saith the Lord.

Therefore if thine enemy hunger, feed him; if he thirst, give him drink: for in so doing thou shalt heap coals of fire on his head.

Be not overcome of evil, but overcome evil with good.

Ephesians 4:32

And be ye kind one to another, tenderhearted, forgiving one another, even as God for Christ's sake hath forgiven you.

Colossians 3:13

Forbearing one another, and forgiving one another, if any man have a quarrel against any: even as Christ forgave you, so also do ye.

1 Peter 3:9

Not rendering evil for evil, or railing for railing: but contrariwise blessing; knowing that ye are thereunto called, that ye should inherit a blessing.

21

FRUSTRATION

Frustrated people often find it easier to throw in the towel and give up. They usually speak first and think later, creating pain for themselves and those with whom they have a connection. Frustration and stress feed each other. We need to stop the vicious cycle by de-stressing our lives.

Deuteronomy 28:20

The LORD shall send upon thee cursing, vexation, and rebuke, in all that thou settest thine hand unto for to do, until thou be destroyed, and until thou perish quickly; because of the wickedness of thy doings, whereby thou hast forsaken me.

Psalms 88:9-13

Mine eye mourneth by reason of affliction: LORD, I have called daily upon thee, I have stretched out my hands unto thee.

Wilt thou shew wonders to the dead? shall the dead arise and praise thee? Selah.

Shall thy lovingkindness be declared in the grave? or thy faithfulness in destruction?

Shall thy wonders be known in the dark? and thy righteousness in the land of forgetfulness?

But unto thee have I cried, O LORD; and in the morning shall my prayer prevent thee.

Psalms 106:23-29

Therefore he said that he would destroy them, had not Moses his chosen stood before him in the breach, to turn away his wrath, lest he should destroy them.

Yea, they despised the pleasant land, they believed not his word:

But murmured in their tents, and hearkened not unto the voice of the LORD.

Therefore he lifted up his hand against them, to overthrow them in the wilderness:

To overthrow their seed also among the nations, and to scatter them in the lands.

They joined themselves also unto Baalpeor, and ate the sacrifices of the dead.

Thus they provoked him to anger with their inventions: and the plague brake in upon them.

Proverbs 11:23

The desire of the righteous is only good: but the expectation of the wicked is wrath.

Ecclesiastes 5:16-17

And this also is a sore evil, that in all points as he came, so shall he go: and what profit hath he that hath laboured for the wind?

All his days also he eateth in darkness, and he hath much sorrow and wrath with his sickness.

1 Peter 5:6-7

Humble yourselves therefore under the mighty hand of God, that he may exalt you in due time:

Casting all your care upon him; for he careth for you.

22

HABITS

As a rule, successful people are no more intelligent than non-successful people are. The reason they are successful is that they have established good habits that generate success. When good habits are developed, The Law of Displacement eradicates any bad habits. Developing good habits will help us remove the stress, depression, and burnout from our lives.

Numbers 33:50-53

And the LORD spake unto Moses in the plains of Moab by Jordan near Jericho, saying,

Speak unto the children of Israel, and say unto them, When ye are passed over Jordan into the land of Canaan;

Then ye shall drive out all the inhabitants of the land from before you, and destroy all their pictures, and destroy all their molten images, and quite pluck down all their high places:

And ye shall dispossess the inhabitants of the land, and dwell therein: for I have given you the land to possess it.

Deuteronomy 7:1-2

When the LORD thy God shall bring thee into the land whither thou goest to possess it, and hath cast out many nations before thee, the Hittites, and the Girgashites, and the Amorites, and the Canaanites, and the Perizzites, and the Hivites, and the Jebusites, seven nations greater and mightier than thou;

And when the LORD thy God shall deliver them before thee; thou shalt smite them, and utterly destroy them; thou shalt make no covenant with them, nor shew mercy unto them.

Job 1:5

And it was so, when the days of their feasting were gone about, that Job sent and sanctified them, and rose up early in the morning, and offered burnt offerings according to the number of them all: for Job said, It may be that my sons have sinned, and cursed God in their hearts. Thus did Job continually.

Psalms 5:3

My voice shalt thou hear in the morning, O LORD; in the morning will I direct my prayer unto thee, and will look up.

Psalms 119:164

Seven times a day do I praise thee because of thy righteous judgments.

Proverbs 18:21

Death and life are in the power of the tongue: and they that love it shall eat the fruit thereof.

Matthew 12:34

O generation of vipers, how can ye, being evil, speak good things? for out of the abundance of the heart the mouth speaketh.

Luke 4:16

And he came to Nazareth, where he had been brought up: and, as his custom was, he went into the synagogue on the sabbath day, and stood up for to read.

Luke 21:34

And take heed to yourselves, lest at any time your hearts be overcharged with surfeiting, and drunkenness, and cares of this life, and so that day come upon you unawares.

John 10:10

The thief cometh not, but for to steal, and to kill, and to destroy: I am come that they might have life, and that they might have it more abundantly.

Romans 12:2

And be not conformed to this world: but be ye transformed by the renewing of your mind, that ye may prove what is that good, and acceptable, and perfect, will of God.

1 Corinthians 14:33

For God is not the author of confusion, but of peace, as in all churches of the saints.

Galatians 5:16

This I say then, Walk in the Spirit, and ye shall not fulfil the lust of the flesh.

Ephesians 1:4-5

According as he hath chosen us in him before the foundation of the world, that we should be holy and without blame before him in love:

Having predestinated us unto the adoption of children by Jesus Christ to himself, according to the good pleasure of his will.

Colossians 4:5

Walk in wisdom toward them that are without, redeeming the time.

23

HEALTH

Stress plays a major role in the top six medical causes of death. We all could live longer if we would take necessary steps to remove stress from our lives. God created us to live one life on this earth. Reincarnation does not exist. Therefore, we get one shot. Choose to live a long, healthy life.

Joshua 14:11

As yet I am as strong this day as I was in the day that Moses sent me: as my strength was then, even so is my strength now, for war, both to go out, and to come in.

Psalms 91:5-6

Thou shalt not be afraid for the terror by night; nor for the arrow that flieth by day;

Nor for the pestilence that walketh in darkness; nor for the destruction that wasteth at noonday.

Psalms 103:2-3

Bless the LORD, O my soul, and forget not all his benefits:

Who forgiveth all thine iniquities; who healeth all thy diseases;

Proverbs 3:7-8

Be not wise in thine own eyes: fear the LORD, and depart from evil.

It shall be health to thy navel, and marrow to thy bones.

Proverbs 4:20-22

My son, attend to my words; incline thine ear unto my sayings.

Let them not depart from thine eyes; keep them in the midst of thine heart.

For they are life unto those that find them, and health to all their flesh.

Isaiah 33:24

And the inhabitant shall not say, I am sick: the people that dwell therein shall be forgiven their iniquity.

Isaiah 53:5

But he was wounded for our transgressions, he was bruised for our iniquities: the chastisement of our peace was upon him; and with his stripes we are healed.

Isaiah 58:8

Then shall thy light break forth as the morning, and thine health shall spring forth speedily: and thy righteousness shall go before thee; the glory of the LORD shall be thy rereward.

Romans 12:1

I beseech you therefore, brethren, by the mercies of God, that ye present your bodies a living sacrifice, holy, acceptable unto God, which is your reasonable service.

1 Corinthians 3:16

Know ye not that ye are the temple of God, and that the Spirit of God dwelleth in you?

Ephesians 5:29

For no man ever yet hated his own flesh; but nourisheth and cherisheth it, even as the Lord the church.

1 Timothy 4:8

For bodily exercise profiteth little: but godliness is profitable unto all things, having promise of the life that now is, and of that which is to come.

3 John 1:2

Beloved, I wish above all things that thou mayest prosper and be in health, even as thy soul prospereth.

24

HONESTY

Honesty is vital. Unfortunately, many only want it when it benefits them. If we plan our lives around honesty, we become less stressful. Stress finds its way into our lives when we operate outside of honesty, because it becomes hard to remember what we previously said or did. Be committed to honesty and alleviate some of the stress.

Deuteronomy 25:15

But thou shalt have a perfect and just weight, a perfect and just measure shalt thou have: that thy days may be lengthened in the land which the Lord thy God giveth thee.

Psalms 7:3-5

O Lord my God, if I have done this; if there be iniquity in my hands;

If I have rewarded evil unto him that was at peace with me; (yea, I have delivered him that without cause is mine enemy:)

Let the enemy persecute my soul, and take it; yea, let him tread down my life upon the earth, and lay mine honour in the dust. Selah.

Psalms 24:3-4

Who shall ascend into the hill of the Lord? or who shall stand in his holy place?

He that hath clean hands, and a pure heart; who hath not lifted up his soul unto vanity, nor sworn deceitfully.

Psalms 25:21

Let integrity and uprightness preserve me; for I wait on thee.

Proverbs 2:7

He layeth up sound wisdom for the righteous: he is a buckler to them that walk uprightly.

Proverbs 4:25-26

Let thine eyes look right on, and let thine eyelids look straight before thee.

Ponder the path of thy feet, and let all thy ways be established.

Proverbs 10:9

He that walketh uprightly walketh surely: but he that perverteth his ways shall be known.

Proverbs 11:1

A false balance is abomination to the Lord: but a just weight is his delight.

Proverbs 11:3

The integrity of the upright shall guide them: but the perverseness of transgressors shall destroy them.

Proverbs 20:10

Divers weights, and divers measures, both of them are alike abomination to the Lord.

Proverbs 20:23

Divers weights are an abomination unto the Lord; and a false balance is not good.

Matthew 7:12

Therefore all things whatsoever ye would that men should do to you, do ye even so to them: for this is the law and the prophets.

Mark 10:19

Thou knowest the commandments, Do not commit adultery, Do not kill, Do not steal, Do not bear false witness, Defraud not, Honour thy father and mother.

Luke 3:13

And he said unto them, Exact no more than that which is appointed you.

Romans 12:17

Recompense to no man evil for evil. Provide things honest in the sight of all men.

2 Corinthians 8:21

Providing for honest things, not only in the sight of the Lord, but also in the sight of men.

Philippians 4:8

Finally, brethren, whatsoever things are true, whatsoever things are honest, whatsoever things are just, whatsoever things are pure, whatsoever things are lovely, whatsoever things are of good report; if there be any virtue, and if there be any praise, think on these things.

1 Thessalonians 4:11-12

And that ye study to be quiet, and to do your own business, and to work with your own hands, as we commanded you;

That ye may walk honestly toward them that are without, and that ye may have lack of nothing.

Hebrews 13:18

Pray for us: for we trust we have a good conscience, in all things willing to live honestly.

1 Peter 2:12

Having your conversation honest among the Gentiles: that, whereas they speak against you as evildoers, they may by your good works, which they shall behold, glorify God in the day of visitation.

25

HOPE

Hope gives us the courage to hang on regardless of what may be happening around us or to us. Hope gives faith a handle on which to grab hold. It will cause a cancer patient to fight to live, believing for a cure. Hope will infuse a jobless person with the desire to look again. It will inspire an abused woman to give love another chance. Hope is a powerful weapon against stress, depression, and burnout.

Psalms 9:18

For the needy shall not alway be forgotten: the expectation of the poor shall not perish for ever.

Psalms 16:9

Therefore my heart is glad, and my glory rejoiceth: my flesh also shall rest in hope.

Psalms 31:24

Be of good courage, and he shall strengthen your heart, all ye that hope in the LORD.

Psalms 33:18

Behold, the eye of the LORD is upon them that fear him, upon them that hope in his mercy.

Psalms 33:22

Let thy mercy, O LORD, be upon us, according as we hope in thee.

Psalms 38:15

For in thee, O LORD, do I hope: thou wilt hear, O Lord my God.

Psalms 39:7

And now, Lord, what wait I for? my hope is in thee.

Psalms 43:5

Why art thou cast down, O my soul? and why art thou disquieted within me? hope in God: for I shall yet praise him, who is the health of my countenance, and my God.

Psalms 71:14

But I will hope continually, and will yet praise thee more and more.

Psalms 119:43

And take not the word of truth utterly out of my mouth; for I have hoped in thy judgments.

Psalms 119:116

Uphold me according unto thy word, that I may live: and let me not be ashamed of my hope.

Psalms 146:5

Happy is he that hath the God of Jacob for his help, whose hope is in the LORD his God.

Proverbs 10:28

The hope of the righteous shall be gladness: but the expectation of the wicked shall perish.

Proverbs 13:12

Hope deferred maketh the heart sick: but when the desire cometh, it is a tree of life.

Proverbs 23:18

For surely there is an end; and thine expectation shall not be cut off.

Ecclesiastes 9:4

For to him that is joined to all the living there is hope: for a living dog is better than a dead lion.

Jeremiah 17:7

Blessed is the man that trusteth in the LORD, and whose hope the LORD is.

Romans 4:18

Who against hope believed in hope, that he might become the father of many nations, according to that which was spoken, So shall thy seed be.

Romans 8:28

And we know that all things work together for good to them that love God, to them who are the called according to his purpose.

Romans 15:13

Now the God of hope fill you with all joy and peace in believing, that ye may abound in hope, through the power of the Holy Ghost.

Galatians 5:5

For we through the Spirit wait for the hope of righteousness by faith.

2 Thessalonians 2:16

Now our Lord Jesus Christ himself, and God, even our Father, which hath loved us, and hath given us everlasting consolation and good hope through grace

Hebrews 11:1

Now faith is the substance of things hoped for, the evidence of things not seen.

1 Peter 1:21

Who by him do believe in God, that raised him up from the dead, and gave him glory; that your faith and hope might be in God.

26

JOY

Although we often use them interchangeably, we should not confuse happiness with joy. Happiness depends upon outside circumstances, but joy is internal. Circumstances will often stress us and thereby affect our happiness. However, joy is a fruit of the Spirit and can remain regardless of what is transpiring around us.

Nehemiah 8:10

Then he said unto them, Go your way, eat the fat, and drink the sweet, and send portions unto them for whom nothing is prepared: for this day is holy unto our Lord: neither be ye sorry; for the joy of the Lord is your strength.

Psalms 2:11

Serve the Lord with fear, and rejoice with trembling.

Psalms 5:11

But let all those that put their trust in thee rejoice: let them ever shout for joy, because thou defendest them: let them also that love thy name be joyful in thee.

Psalms 9:2

I will be glad and rejoice in thee: I will sing praise to thy name, O thou most High.

Psalms 16:9

Therefore my heart is glad, and my glory rejoiceth: my flesh also shall rest in hope.

Psalms 16:11

Thou wilt shew me the path of life: in thy presence is fulness of joy; at thy right hand there are pleasures for evermore.

Psalms 30:5

For his anger endureth but a moment; in his favour is life: weeping may endure for a night, but joy cometh in the morning.

Psalms 32:11

Be glad in the Lord, and rejoice, ye righteous: and shout for joy, all ye that are upright in heart.

Psalms 35:9

And my soul shall be joyful in the Lord: it shall rejoice in his salvation.

Psalms 42:4

When I remember these things, I pour out my soul in me: for I had gone with the multitude, I went with them to the house of God, with the voice of joy and praise , with a multitude that kept holyday.

Psalms 43:4

Then will I go unto the altar of God, unto God my exceeding joy: yea, upon the harp will I praise thee, O God my God.

Psalms 51:12

Restore unto me the joy of thy salvation; and uphold me with thy free spirit.

Psalms 100:1

Make a joyful noise unto the Lord, all ye lands.

Psalms 126:5

They that sow in tears shall reap in joy.

Isaiah 29:19

The meek also shall increase their joy in the Lord, and the poor among men shall rejoice in the Holy One of Israel.

Isaiah 51:11

Therefore the redeemed of the Lord shall return, and come with singing unto Zion; and everlasting joy shall be upon their head: they shall obtain gladness and joy; and sorrow and mourning shall flee away.

Habakkuk 3:18

Yet I will rejoice in the Lord, I will joy in the God of my salvation.

John 16:22

And ye now therefore have sorrow: but I will see you again, and your heart shall rejoice, and your joy no man taketh from you.

John 16:24

Hitherto have ye asked nothing in my name: ask, and ye shall receive, that your joy may be full.

Romans 14:17

For the kingdom of God is not meat and drink; but righteousness, and peace, and joy in the Holy Ghost.

Romans 15:13

Now the God of hope fill you with all joy and peace in believing, that ye may abound in hope, through the power of the Holy Ghost.

Galatians 5:22

But the fruit of the Spirit is love, joy, peace, longsuffering, gentleness, goodness, faith.

Ephesians 5:18-19

And be not drunk with wine, wherein is excess; but be filled with the Spirit;

Speaking to yourselves in psalms and hymns and spiritual songs, singing and making melody in your heart to the Lord.

1 Thessalonians 5:16

Rejoice evermore.

James 1:2

My brethren, count it all joy when ye fall into divers temptations.

1 John 1:4

And these things write we unto you, that your joy may be full.

27

LAUGHTER

God wants us to laugh. According to Psalms 2:1ff, God laughs; and since he created us in His image, we should laugh. There are at least thirteen direct benefits of laughter. It elevates moods, and lowers blood pressure. However, most importantly, it greatly reduces stress and the negative effects it has in our lives.

Genesis 21:6

And Sarah said, God hath made me to laugh, so that all that hear will laugh with me.

Job 8:20-21

Behold, God will not cast away a perfect man, neither will he help the evil doers:

Till he fill thy mouth with laughing, and thy lips with rejoicing.

Job 22:19

The righteous see it, and are glad: and the innocent laugh them to scorn.

Psalms 2:4

He that sitteth in the heavens shall laugh: the Lord shall have them in derision.

Psalms 16:9

Therefore my heart is glad, and my glory rejoiceth: my flesh also shall rest in hope.

Psalms 128:1-2

Blessed is every one that feareth the LORD; that walketh in his ways.

For thou shalt eat the labour of thine hands: happy shalt thou be, and it shall be well with thee.

Proverbs 15:13

A merry heart maketh a cheerful countenance: but by sorrow of the heart the spirit is broken.

Proverbs 15:15

All the days of the afflicted are evil: but he that is of a merry heart hath a continual feast.

Proverbs 17:22

A merry heart doeth good like a medicine: but a broken spirit drieth the bones.

Ecclesiastes 3:4

A time to weep, and a time to laugh; a time to mourn, and a time to dance.

Luke 6:21

Blessed are ye that hunger now: for ye shall be filled. Blessed are ye that weep now: for ye shall laugh.

Romans 14:17

For the kingdom of God is not meat and drink; but righteousness, and peace, and joy in the Holy Ghost.

2 Corinthians 1:12

For our rejoicing is this, the testimony of our conscience, that in simplicity and godly sincerity, not with fleshly wisdom, but by the grace of God, we have had our conversation in the world, and more abundantly to you-ward.

28

LOYALTY

One of the most important characteristics of those, whom we allow in our circle, should be loyalty. Someone who is loyal is willing to make personal sacrifices to ensure the strength of the friendship. When loyal people connect with us, it frees us from some of the burden that causes stress, depression, and burnout in our lives.

Proverbs 3:3

Let not mercy and truth forsake thee: bind them about thy neck; write them upon the table of thine heart.

Proverbs 20:6

Most men will proclaim every one his own goodness: but a faithful man who can find?

Proverbs 20:28

Mercy and truth preserve the king: and his throne is upholden by mercy.

Proverbs 21:21

He that followeth after righteousness and mercy findeth life, righteousness, and honour.

Ecclesiastes 8:2-3

I counsel thee to keep the king's commandment, and that in regard of the oath of God.

Be not hasty to go out of his sight: stand not in an evil thing; for he doeth whatsoever pleaseth him.

Ecclesiastes 10:4

If the spirit of the ruler rise up against thee, leave not thy place; for yielding pacifieth great offences.

Matthew 6:33

But seek ye first the kingdom of God, and his righteousness; and all these things shall be added unto you.

1 Corinthians 10:21

Ye cannot drink the cup of the Lord, and the cup of devils: ye cannot be partakers of the Lord's table, and of the table of devils.

Let the wife make the husband glad to come home, and let him make her sorry to see him leave.

— Martin Luther

29

MARRIAGE

Marriage is God-ordained and God-instituted. Before there was the Church, there was marriage. Stress, depression, and burnout weigh heavily upon the marital relationship. However, a biblically strong marriage can lessen the effects of the stress and make it more manageable.

Genesis 2:21-24

And the LORD God caused a deep sleep to fall upon Adam, and he slept: and he took one of his ribs, and closed up the flesh instead thereof;

And the rib, which the LORD God had taken from man, made he a woman, and brought her unto the man.

And Adam said, This is now bone of my bones, and flesh of my flesh: she shall be called Woman, because she was taken out of Man.

Therefore shall a man leave his father and his mother, and shall cleave unto his wife: and they shall be one flesh.

Proverbs 5:15-20

Drink waters out of thine own cistern, and running waters out of thine own well.

Let thy fountains be dispersed abroad, and rivers of waters in the streets.

Let them be only thine own, and not strangers' with thee.

Let thy fountain be blessed: and rejoice with the wife of thy youth.

Let her be as the loving hind and pleasant roe; let her breasts satisfy thee at all times; and be thou ravished always with her love.

And why wilt thou, my son, be ravished with a strange woman, and embrace the bosom of a stranger?

Proverbs 18:22

Whoso findeth a wife findeth a good thing, and obtaineth favour of the LORD.

Song of Solomon 4:9-12

Thou hast ravished my heart, my sister, my spouse; thou hast ravished my heart with one of thine eyes, with one chain of thy neck.

How fair is thy love, my sister, my spouse! how much better is thy love than wine! and the smell of thine ointments than all spices!

Thy lips, O my spouse, drop as the honeycomb: honey and milk are under thy tongue; and the smell of thy garments is like the smell of Lebanon.

A garden inclosed is my sister, my spouse; a spring shut up, a fountain sealed.

Malachi 2:14

Yet ye say, Wherefore? Because the LORD hath been witness between thee and the wife of thy youth, against whom thou hast dealt treacherously: yet is she thy companion, and the wife of thy covenant.

Matthew 5:31-32

It hath been said, Whosoever shall put away his wife, let him give her a writing of divorcement:

But I say unto you, That whosoever shall put away his wife, saving for the cause of fornication, causeth her to commit adultery: and whosoever shall marry her that is divorced committeth adultery.

Romans 7:1-3

Know ye not, brethren, (for I speak to them that know the law,) how that the law hath dominion over a man as long as he liveth?

For the woman which hath an husband is bound by the law to her husband so long as he liveth; but if the husband be dead, she is loosed from the law of her husband.

So then if, while her husband liveth, she be married to another man, she shall be called an adulteress: but if her husband be dead, she is free from that law; so that she is no adulteress, though she be married to another man.

1 Corinthians 7:2

Nevertheless, to avoid fornication, let every man have his own wife, and let every woman have her own husband.

1 Corinthians 11:11

Nevertheless neither is the man without the woman, neither the woman without the man, in the Lord.

Ephesians 5:22-25

Wives, submit yourselves unto your own husbands, as unto the Lord.

For the husband is the head of the wife, even as Christ is the head of the church: and he is the saviour of the body.

Therefore as the church is subject unto Christ, so let the wives be to their own husbands in every thing.

Husbands, love your wives, even as Christ also loved the church, and gave himself for it.

Hebrews 13:4

Marriage is honourable in all, and the bed undefiled: but whoremongers and adulterers God will judge.

30

MONEY/WEALTH

Someone once said, *"Money makes the world go around."* Money may not make someone happy, but it goes a long way to calm our anxieties. Money is neither good nor bad – it all depends on how we manage it. Lack of money greatly affects our level of stress.

Genesis 13:2

And Abram was very rich in cattle, in silver, and in gold.

Deuteronomy 1:11

(The Lord God of your fathers make you a thousand times so many more as ye are, and bless you, as he hath promised you!)

Deuteronomy 6:10-12

And it shall be, when the Lord thy God shall have brought thee into the land which he sware unto thy fathers, to Abraham, to Isaac, and to Jacob, to give thee great and goodly cities, which thou buildedst not,

And houses full of all good things, which thou filledst not, and wells digged, which thou diggedst not, vineyards and olive trees, which thou plantedst not; when thou shalt have eaten and be full;

Then beware lest thou forget the Lord, which brought thee forth out of the land of Egypt, from the house of bondage.

Joshua 1:8

This book of the law shall not depart out of thy mouth; but thou shalt meditate therein day and night, that thou mayest observe to do according to all that is written therein: for then thou shalt make thy way prosperous, and then thou shalt have good success.

Job 22:23-27

If thou return to the Almighty, thou shalt be built up, thou shalt put away iniquity far from thy tabernacles.

Then shalt thou lay up gold as dust, and the gold of Ophir as the stones of the brooks.

Yea, the Almighty shall be thy defence, and thou shalt have plenty of silver.

For then shalt thou have thy delight in the Almighty, and shalt lift up thy face unto God.

Thou shalt make thy prayer unto him, and he shall hear thee, and thou shalt pay thy vows.

Job 42:11

Then came there unto him all his brethren, and all his sisters, and all they that had been of his acquaintance before, and did eat bread with him in his house: and they bemoaned him, and comforted him over all the evil that the Lord had brought upon him: every man also gave him a piece of money, and every one an earring of gold.

Psalms 1:3

And he shall be like a tree planted by the rivers of water, that bringeth forth his fruit in his season; his leaf also shall not wither; and whatsoever he doeth shall prosper.

Psalms 37:16

A little that a righteous man hath is better than the riches of many wicked.

Psalms 37:21

The wicked borroweth, and payeth not again: but the righteous sheweth mercy, and giveth.

Psalms 128:1-2

Blessed is every one that feareth the Lord; that walketh in his ways.

For thou shalt eat the labour of thine hands: happy shalt thou be, and it shall be well with thee.

Proverbs 10:22

The blessing of the Lord, it maketh rich, and he addeth no sorrow with it.

Proverbs 14:24

The crown of the wise is their riches: but the foolishness of fools is folly.

Proverbs 15:6

In the house of the righteous is much treasure: but in the revenues of the wicked is trouble.

Proverbs 18:11

The rich man's wealth is his strong city, and as an high wall in his own conceit.

Proverbs 19:4

Wealth maketh many friends; but the poor is separated from his neighbour.

Proverbs 21:20

There is treasure to be desired and oil in the dwelling of the wise; but a foolish man spendeth it up.

Proverbs 28:20

A faithful man shall abound with blessings: but he that maketh haste to be rich shall not be innocent.

Ecclesiastes 5:9

Moreover the profit of the earth is for all: the king himself is served by the field.

Ecclesiastes 7:11-12

Wisdom is good with an inheritance: and by it there is profit to them that see the sun.

For wisdom is a defence, and money is a defence: but the excellency of knowledge is, that wisdom giveth life to them that have it.

Ecclesiastes 10:19

A feast is made for laughter, and wine maketh merry: but money answereth all things.

Hosea 12:8

And Ephraim said, Yet I am become rich, I have found me out substance: in all my labours they shall find none iniquity in me that were sin.

Luke 12:15

And he said unto them, Take heed, and beware of covetousness: for a man's life consisteth not in the abundance of the things which he possesseth.

1 Timothy 6:10

For the love of money is the root of all evil: which while some coveted after, they have erred from the faith, and pierced themselves through with many sorrows.

1 Timothy 6:17-19

Charge them that are rich in this world, that they be not highminded, nor trust in uncertain riches, but in the living God, who giveth us richly all things to enjoy;

That they do good, that they be rich in good works, ready to distribute, willing to communicate;

Laying up in store for themselves a good foundation against the time to come, that they may lay hold on eternal life.

3 John 1:2

Beloved, I wish above all things that thou mayest prosper and be in health, even as thy soul prospereth.

Obedience is
the mother of
success and is
wedded to
safety.

— Aeschylus

31

OBEDIENCE

Obedience brings peace. It makes for a smoother life. Children often have trouble at home because they simply have an obedience problem. Christians encounter most of their problems simply because they will not obey God's commands for their lives. When we learn to obey the voice of God and those who have rule over us, our lives will become much smoother, including less stress.

Genesis 2:16-17

And the Lord God commanded the man, saying, Of every tree of the garden thou mayest freely eat:

But of the tree of the knowledge of good and evil, thou shalt not eat of it: for in the day that thou eatest thereof thou shalt surely die.

Genesis 17:9

And God said unto Abraham, Thou shalt keep my covenant therefore, thou, and thy seed after thee in their generations.

Exodus 15:26

And said, If thou wilt diligently hearken to the voice of the Lord thy God, and wilt do that which is right in his sight, and wilt give ear to his commandments, and keep all his statutes, I will put none of these diseases upon thee, which I have brought upon the Egyptians: for I am the Lord that healeth thee.

Joshua 1:6-8

Be strong and of a good courage: for unto this people shalt thou divide for an inheritance the land, which I sware unto their fathers to give them.

Only be thou strong and very courageous, that thou mayest observe to do according to all the law, which Moses my servant commanded thee: turn not from it to the right hand or to the left, that thou mayest prosper whithersoever thou goest.

This book of the law shall not depart out of thy mouth; but thou shalt meditate therein day and night, that thou mayest observe to do according to all that is written therein: for then thou shalt make thy way prosperous, and then thou shalt have good success.

1 Samuel 15:22

And Samuel said, Hath the Lord as great delight in burnt offerings and sacrifices, as in obeying the voice of the Lord? Behold, to obey is better than sacrifice, and to hearken than the fat of rams.

Nehemiah 1:5

And said, I beseech thee, O Lord God of heaven, the great and terrible God, that keepeth covenant and mercy for them that love him and observe his commandments.

Psalms 1:1-2

Blessed is the man that walketh not in the counsel of the ungodly, nor standeth in the way of sinners, nor sitteth in the seat of the scornful.

But his delight is in the law of the Lord; and in his law doth he meditate day and night.

Psalms 103:17-18

But the mercy of the Lord is from everlasting to everlasting upon them that fear him, and his righteousness unto children's children;

To such as keep his covenant, and to those that remember his commandments to do them.

Psalms 111:10

The fear of the Lord is the beginning of wisdom: a good understanding have all they that do his commandments: his praise endureth for ever.

Psalms 119:15-16

I will meditate in thy precepts, and have respect unto thy ways.

I will delight myself in thy statutes: I will not forget thy word.

Psalms 119:60

I made haste, and delayed not to keep thy commandments.

Proverbs 19:16

He that keepeth the commandment keepeth his own soul; but he that despiseth his ways shall die.

Proverbs 28:7

Whoso keepeth the law is a wise son: but he that is a companion of riotous men shameth his father.

Isaiah 1:19

If ye be willing and obedient, ye shall eat the good of the land.

Isaiah 50:10

Who is among you that feareth the Lord, that obeyeth the voice of his servant, that walketh in darkness, and hath no light? let him trust in the name of the Lord, and stay upon his God.

Jeremiah 7:23

But this thing commanded I them, saying, Obey my voice, and I will be your God, and ye shall be my people: and walk ye in all the ways that I have commanded you, that it may be well unto you.

Luke 8:21

And he answered and said unto them, My mother and my brethren are these which hear the word of God, and do it.

Luke 11:28

But he said, Yea rather, blessed are they that hear the word of God, and keep it.

John 13:17

If ye know these things, happy are ye if ye do them.

Romans 13:1-4

Let every soul be subject unto the higher powers. For there is no power but of God: the powers that be are ordained of God.

Whosoever therefore resisteth the power, resisteth the ordinance of God: and they that resist shall receive to themselves damnation.

For rulers are not a terror to good works, but to the evil. Wilt thou then not be afraid of the power? do that which is good, and thou shalt have praise of the same:

For he is the minister of God to thee for good. But if thou do that which is evil, be afraid; for he beareth not the sword in vain: for he is the minister of God, a revenger to execute wrath upon him that doeth evil.

Hebrews 13:7

Remember them which have the rule over you, who have spoken unto you the word of God: whose faith follow, considering the end of their conversation.

Hebrews 13:17

Obey them that have the rule over you, and submit yourselves: for they watch for your souls, as they that must give account, that they may do it with joy, and not with grief: for that is unprofitable for you.

The first recipe
for happiness
is: avoid too
lengthy
meditation on
the past.

— Andre Maurois

32

THE PAST

The greatest hindrance to today's blessings is yesterday's blessings. Those who are constantly looking behind them walk past what God has prepared for them today. If the past was good, thank God for it and move forward. If the past was bad, you cannot change it – keep moving forward until today's blessings erase yesterday's pain. Do not lived stressed out over what you cannot change.

Genesis 19:26

But his wife looked back from behind him, and she became a pillar of salt.

Ecclesiastes 1:9-11

The thing that hath been, it is that which shall be; and that which is done is that which shall be done: and there is no new thing under the sun.

Is there any thing whereof it may be said, See, this is new? it hath been already of old time, which was before us.

There is no remembrance of former things; neither shall there be any remembrance of things that are to come with those that shall come after.

Luke 9:62

And Jesus said unto him, No man, having put his hand to the plough, and looking back, is fit for the kingdom of God.

Philippians 3:8

Yea doubtless, and I count all things but loss for the excellency of the knowledge of Christ Jesus my Lord: for whom I have suffered the loss of all things, and do count them but dung, that I may win Christ.

Philippians 3:12-14

Not as though I had already attained, either were already perfect: but I follow after, if that I may apprehend that for which also I am apprehended of Christ Jesus.

Brethren, I count not myself to have apprehended: but this one thing I do, forgetting those things which are behind, and reaching forth unto those things which are before,

I press toward the mark for the prize of the high calling of God in Christ Jesus.

Hebrews 6:1

Therefore leaving the principles of the doctrine of Christ, let us go on unto perfection; not laying again the foundation of repentance from dead works, and of faith toward God

*Peace is its
own reward.*

— *Mahatma Gandhi*

33

PEACE

The absence of peace is turmoil. When the sea and wind were raging, those on board the ship feared for their lives. However, when Jesus brought peace to the situation, fear departed. Stress and lack of peace feast upon each other. When we bring peace into our lives, it helps starve the stress.

Leviticus 26:6

And I will give peace in the land, and ye shall lie down, and none shall make you afraid: and I will rid evil beasts out of the land, neither shall the sword go through your land.

Job 5:23-24

For thou shalt be in league with the stones of the field: and the beasts of the field shall be at peace with thee.

And thou shalt know that thy tabernacle shall be in peace; and thou shalt visit thy habitation, and shalt not sin.

Psalms 29:11

The LORD will give strength unto his people; the LORD will bless his people with peace.

Psalms 34:14

Depart from evil, and do good; seek peace, and pursue it.

Psalms 37:11

But the meek shall inherit the earth; and shall delight themselves in the abundance of peace.

Psalms 37:37

Mark the perfect man, and behold the upright: for the end of that man is peace.

Psalms 119:165

Great peace have they which love thy law: and nothing shall offend them.

Psalms 120:6-7

My soul hath long dwelt with him that hateth peace.

I am for peace: but when I speak, they are for war.

Psalms 133:1

Behold, how good and how pleasant it is for brethren to dwell together in unity!

Proverbs 12:20

Deceit is in the heart of them that imagine evil: but to the counsellors of peace is joy.

Proverbs 16:7

When a man's ways please the LORD, he maketh even his enemies to be at peace with him.

Ecclesiastes 4:6

Better is an handful with quietness, than both the hands full with travail and vexation of spirit.

Isaiah 45:7

I form the light, and create darkness: I make peace, and create evil: I the LORD do all these things.

Isaiah 48:22

There is no peace, saith the LORD, unto the wicked.

Isaiah 53:5

But he was wounded for our transgressions, he was bruised for our iniquities: the chastisement of our peace was upon him; and with his stripes we are healed.

Matthew 5:9

Blessed are the peacemakers: for they shall be called the children of God.

Matthew 5:23-24

Therefore if thou bring thy gift to the altar, and there rememberest that thy brother hath ought against thee;

Leave there thy gift before the altar, and go thy way; first be reconciled to thy brother, and then come and offer thy gift.

Mark 9:50

Salt is good: but if the salt have lost his saltness, wherewith will ye season it? Have salt in yourselves, and have peace one with another.

Romans 12:18

If it be possible, as much as lieth in you, live peaceably with all men.

Romans 14:19

Let us therefore follow after the things which make for peace, and things wherewith one may edify another.

1 Corinthians 14:33

For God is not the author of confusion, but of peace, as in all churches of the saints.

2 Corinthians 13:11

Finally, brethren, farewell. Be perfect, be of good comfort, be of one mind, live in peace; and the God of love and peace shall be with you.

Ephesians 4:3

Endeavouring to keep the unity of the Spirit in the bond of peace.

1 Thessalonians 5:13

And to esteem them very highly in love for their work's sake. And be at peace among yourselves.

1 Timothy 2:1-2

I exhort therefore, that, first of all, supplications, prayers, intercessions, and giving of thanks, be made for all men;

For kings, and for all that are in authority; that we may lead a quiet and peaceable life in all godliness and honesty.

2 Timothy 2:22

Flee also youthful lusts: but follow righteousness, faith, charity, peace, with them that call on the Lord out of a pure heart.

Hebrews 12:14

Follow peace with all men, and holiness, without which no man shall see the Lord:

James 3:17-18

But the wisdom that is from above is first pure, then peaceable, gentle, and easy to be intreated, full of mercy and good fruits, without partiality, and without hypocrisy.

And the fruit of righteousness is sown in peace of them that make peace.

1 Peter 3:10-11

For he that will love life, and see good days, let him refrain his tongue from evil, and his lips that they speak no guile:

Let him eschew evil, and do good; let him seek peace, and ensue it.

34

PLANNING/GOALS

To succeed there must be planned goals. Without a plan, how will we know if we have made it to our destination? Those who are successful plan their work and work their plan. Stressed, depressed, and burned out people are often that way because they have no plans or goals on which to focus.

Genesis 29:20-28

And Jacob served seven years for Rachel; and they seemed unto him but a few days, for the love he had to her.

And Jacob said unto Laban, Give me my wife, for my days are fulfilled, that I may go in unto her.

And Laban gathered together all the men of the place, and made a feast.

And it came to pass in the evening, that he took Leah his daughter, and brought her to him; and he went in unto her.

And Laban gave unto his daughter Leah Zilpah his maid for an handmaid.

And it came to pass, that in the morning, behold, it was Leah: and he said to Laban, What is this thou hast done unto me? did not I serve with thee for Rachel? wherefore then hast thou beguiled me?

And Laban said, It must not be so done in our country, to give the younger before the firstborn.

Fulfil her week, and we will give thee this also for the service which thou shalt serve with me yet seven other years.

And Jacob did so, and fulfilled her week: and he gave him Rachel his daughter to wife also.

Exodus 25:8-9

And let them make me a sanctuary; that I may dwell among them.

According to all that I shew thee, after the pattern of the tabernacle, and the pattern of all the instruments thereof, even so shall ye make it.

Psalms 97:10

Ye that love the Lord, hate evil: he preserveth the souls of his saints; he delivereth them out of the hand of the wicked.

Proverbs 16:3

Commit thy works unto the Lord, and thy thoughts shall be established.

Proverbs 16:9

A man's heart deviseth his way: but the Lord directeth his steps.

Ecclesiastes 9:10

Whatsoever thy hand findeth to do, do it with thy might; for there is no work, nor device, nor knowledge, nor wisdom, in the grave, whither thou goest.

Jeremiah 29:11

For I know the thoughts that I think toward you, saith the Lord, thoughts of peace, and not of evil, to give you an expected end.

James 4:13-17

Go to now, ye that say, To day or to morrow we will go into such a city, and continue there a year, and buy and sell, and get gain:

Whereas ye know not what shall be on the morrow. For what is your life? It is even a vapour, that appeareth for a little time, and then vanisheth away.

For that ye ought to say, If the Lord will, we shall live, and do this, or that.

But now ye rejoice in your boastings: all such rejoicing is evil.

Therefore to him that knoweth to do good, and doeth it not, to him it is sin.

35

PRAYER

Saints of generations past used to have a saying, *"Pray until you pray through. Prayer changes things."* Prayer is a powerful weapon against the adversary and all of his techniques. Prayer may not prevent stress, if other conditions are present, but prayer will greatly enhance our ability to deal with, and overcome the stress that comes our way.

Psalms 5:3

My voice shalt thou hear in the morning, O LORD; in the morning will I direct my prayer unto thee, and will look up.

Psalms 40:13

Be pleased, O LORD, to deliver me: O LORD, make haste to help me.

Psalms 55:17

Evening, and morning, and at noon, will I pray, and cry aloud: and he shall hear my voice.

Psalms 88:1

O LORD God of my salvation, I have cried day and night before thee

Psalms 88:13

But unto thee have I cried, O LORD; and in the morning shall my prayer prevent thee.

Isaiah 55:6

Seek ye the LORD while he may be found, call ye upon him while he is near

Matthew 6:6

But thou, when thou prayest, enter into thy closet, and when thou hast shut thy door, pray to thy

Father which is in secret; and thy Father which seeth in secret shall reward thee openly.

Matthew 6:9-13

After this manner therefore pray ye: Our Father which art in heaven, Hallowed be thy name.

Thy kingdom come. Thy will be done in earth, as it is in heaven.

Give us this day our daily bread.

And forgive us our debts, as we forgive our debtors.

And lead us not into temptation, but deliver us from evil: For thine is the kingdom, and the power, and the glory, for ever. Amen.

John 16:23-24

And in that day ye shall ask me nothing. Verily, verily, I say unto you, Whatsoever ye shall ask the Father in my name, he will give it you.

Hitherto have ye asked nothing in my name: ask, and ye shall receive, that your joy may be full.

Ephesians 6:18

Praying always with all prayer and supplication in the Spirit, and watching thereunto with all perseverance and supplication for all saints;

James 1:6

But let him ask in faith, nothing wavering. For he that wavereth is like a wave of the sea driven with the wind and tossed.

James 4:3

Ye ask, and receive not, because ye ask amiss, that ye may consume it upon your lusts.

1 John 5:14-15

And this is the confidence that we have in him, that, if we ask any thing according to his will, he heareth us:

And if we know that he hear us, whatsoever we ask, we know that we have the petitions that we desired of him.

36

REST

Everything God created, He created to enjoy seasons of rest. Winter provides time for the fruit trees and plants to rest. He demanded that the land enjoy a year of rest every seven years. He created mankind out of the dirt of the earth, and all dirt must rest. Rested ground produces a better harvest. Taking necessary time to rest reduces stress and lessens the chance of depression and burnout.

Genesis 2:2-3

And on the seventh day God ended his work which he had made; and he rested on the seventh day from all his work which he had made.

And God blessed the seventh day, and sanctified it: because that in it he had rested from all his work which God created and made.

Exodus 20:8

Remember the sabbath day, to keep it holy.

Exodus 20:11

For in six days the Lord made heaven and earth, the sea, and all that in them is, and rested the seventh day: wherefore the Lord blessed the sabbath day, and hallowed it.

Exodus 23:12

Six days thou shalt do thy work, and on the seventh day thou shalt rest: that thine ox and thine ass may rest, and the son of thy handmaid, and the stranger, may be refreshed.

Psalms 23:2

He maketh me to lie down in green pastures: he leadeth me beside the still waters.

Psalms 55:6-8

And I said, Oh that I had wings like a dove! for then would I fly away, and be at rest.

Lo, then would I wander far off, and remain in the wilderness. Selah.

I would hasten my escape from the windy storm and tempest.

Psalms 94:13

That thou mayest give him rest from the days of adversity, until the pit be digged for the wicked.

Psalms 116:7

Return unto thy rest, O my soul; for the Lord hath dealt bountifully with thee.

Ecclesiastes 2:22-23

For what hath man of all his labour, and of the vexation of his heart, wherein he hath laboured under the sun?

For all his days are sorrows, and his travail grief; yea, his heart taketh not rest in the night. This is also vanity.

Isaiah 14:3

And it shall come to pass in the day that the Lord shall give thee rest from thy sorrow, and from thy fear, and from the hard bondage wherein thou wast made to serve.

Isaiah 28:12

To whom he said, This is the rest wherewith ye may cause the weary to rest; and this is the refreshing: yet they would not hear.

Isaiah 30:15

For thus saith the Lord GOD, the Holy One of Israel; In returning and rest shall ye be saved; in quietness and in confidence shall be your strength: and ye would not.

Matthew 11:29

Take my yoke upon you, and learn of me; for I am meek and lowly in heart: and ye shall find rest unto your souls.

Mark 6:31

And he said unto them, Come ye yourselves apart into a desert place, and rest a while: for there were many coming and going, and they had no leisure so much as to eat.

Romans 15:32

That I may come unto you with joy by the will of God, and may with you be refreshed.

2 Thessalonians 1:7

And to you who are troubled rest with us, when the Lord Jesus shall be revealed from heaven with his mighty angels,

Hebrews 4:1-3

Let us therefore fear, lest, a promise being left us of entering into his rest, any of you should seem to come short of it.

For unto us was the gospel preached, as well as unto them: but the word preached did not profit them, not being mixed with faith in them that heard it.

For we which have believed do enter into rest, as he said, As I have sworn in my wrath, if they shall enter into my rest: although the works were finished from the foundation of the world.

37

SELF-CONTROL

Self-control is vital to many areas of our lives – i.e. our health, our money, and our relationships. Studies have proven that people with high degrees of self-control are happier than those who have little or no self-control. To live stress free and avoid depression and burnout, we must develop and practice self-control in our daily lives.

Job 1:20-22

Then Job arose, and rent his mantle, and shaved his head, and fell down upon the ground, and worshipped,

And said, Naked came I out of my mother's womb, and naked shall I return thither: the LORD gave, and the LORD hath taken away; blessed be the name of the LOR

In all this Job sinned not, nor charged God foolishly.

Proverbs 13:3

He that keepeth his mouth keepeth his life: but he that openeth wide his lips shall have destruction.

Proverbs 29:11

A fool uttereth all his mind: but a wise man keepeth it in till afterwards.

1 Corinthians 9:25-27

And every man that striveth for the mastery is temperate in all things. Now they do it to obtain a corruptible crown; but we an incorruptible.

I therefore so run, not as uncertainly; so fight I, not as one that beateth the air:

But I keep under my body, and bring it into subjection: lest that by any means, when I have preached to others, I myself should be a castaway.

Galatians 5:22-23

But the fruit of the Spirit is love, joy, peace, longsuffering, gentleness, goodness, faith,

Meekness, temperance: against such there is no law.

Ephesians 4:26-27

Be ye angry, and sin not: let not the sun go down upon your wrath:

Neither give place to the devil.

2 Peter 1:5-6

And beside this, giving all diligence, add to your faith virtue; and to virtue knowledge;

And to knowledge temperance; and to temperance patience; and to patience godliness

It is easy to look down on others; to look down on ourselves is the difficulty.

— Walter Savage Landor

38

SELF-EXAMINATION

One of the greatest stress multipliers is wondering what others will think of us, and our decisions and actions. To reduce stress in our lives we should examine our motives, our actions, and ourselves. Once we have judged ourselves and understand we did the best we could with what we had, we should not accept the condemnation that others send our way.

Job 13:23

How many are mine iniquities and sins? make me to know my transgression and my sin.

Psalms 4:4

Stand in awe, and sin not: commune with your own heart upon your bed, and be still. Selah.

Psalms 19:12

Who can understand his errors? cleanse thou me from secret faults.

Psalms 26:2

Examine me, O LORD, and prove me; try my reins and my heart.

Psalms 77:6

I call to remembrance my song in the night: I commune with mine own heart: and my spirit made diligent search.

Psalms 119:59

I thought on my ways, and turned my feet unto thy testimonies.

Psalms 139:23-24

Search me, O God, and know my heart: try me, and know my thoughts.

And see if there be any wicked way in me, and lead me in the way everlasting.

Jeremiah 17:9

The heart is deceitful above all things, and desperately wicked: who can know it?

Haggai 1:7

Thus saith the LORD of hosts; Consider your ways.

1 Corinthians 11:28

But let a man examine himself, and so let him eat of that bread, and drink of that cup.

1 Corinthians 11:31

For if we would judge ourselves, we should not be judged.

2 Corinthians 13:5

Examine yourselves, whether ye be in the faith; prove your own selves. Know ye not your own selves, how that Jesus Christ is in you, except ye be reprobates?

Galatians 6:4

But let every man prove his own work, and then shall he have rejoicing in himself alone, and not in another.

39

SPEECH

Words matter. Much of what we experience today is because of the words we spoke yesterday. Unfortunately, we are prone to speak without thinking. As someone once said, *"Don't engage your mouth without first engaging your brain."* The problem with words is, once they are in the atmosphere, they are not retrievable. Loose lips create problems that breed stress.

Job 22:28

Thou shalt also decree a thing, and it shall be established unto thee: and the light shall shine upon thy ways.

Psalms 34:13

Keep thy tongue from evil, and thy lips from speaking guile.

Psalms 37:30

The mouth of the righteous speaketh wisdom, and his tongue talketh of judgment.

Psalms 49:3

My mouth shall speak of wisdom; and the meditation of my heart shall be of understanding.

Psalms 145:21

My mouth shall speak the praise of the Lord: and let all flesh bless his holy name for ever and ever.

Proverbs 6:2

Thou art snared with the words of thy mouth, thou art taken with the words of thy mouth.

Proverbs 10:19

In the multitude of words there wanteth not sin: but he that refraineth his lips is wise.

Proverbs 16:21

The wise in heart shall be called prudent: and the sweetness of the lips increaseth learning.

Proverbs 17:27-28

He that hath knowledge spareth his words: and a man of understanding is of an excellent spirit.

Even a fool, when he holdeth his peace, is counted wise: and he that shutteth his lips is esteemed a man of understanding.

Proverbs 20:15

There is gold, and a multitude of rubies: but the lips of knowledge are a precious jewel.

Zechariah 8:16

These are the things that ye shall do; Speak ye every man the truth to his neighbour; execute the judgment of truth and peace in your gates

Matthew 5:37

But let your communication be, Yea, yea; Nay, nay: for whatsoever is more than these cometh of evil.

Matthew 12:36-37

But I say unto you, That every idle word that men shall speak, they shall give account thereof in the day of judgment.

For by thy words thou shalt be justified, and by thy words thou shalt be condemned.

Ephesians 4:29

Let no corrupt communication proceed out of your mouth, but that which is good to the use of edifying, that it may minister grace unto the hearers.

Colossians 4:6

Let your speech be alway with grace, seasoned with salt, that ye may know how ye ought to answer every man.

2 Timothy 1:13

Hold fast the form of sound words, which thou hast heard of me, in faith and love which is in Christ Jesus.

James 3:5-6

Even so the tongue is a little member, and boasteth great things. Behold, how great a matter a little fire kindleth!

And the tongue is a fire, a world of iniquity: so is the tongue among our members, that it defileth the whole body, and setteth on fire the course of nature; and it is set on fire of hell.

James 5:12

But above all things, my brethren, swear not, neither by heaven, neither by the earth, neither by any other oath: but let your yea be yea; and your nay, nay; lest ye fall into condemnation.

We can no more
do without
spirituality than
we can do
without food,
shelter, or
clothing.

— Ernest Holmes

40

SPIRITUALITY

There are many redeeming qualities of spirituality, apart from the obvious – going to heaven. Experts proved that the more spiritual people are, the healthier they are; the more gracious they become; and the more they flourish. To defeat stress, depression, and burnout, we should make spiritual maturity a priority.

Deuteronomy 6:5

And thou shalt love the Lord thy God with all thine heart, and with all thy soul, and with all thy might.

Joshua 22:5

But take diligent heed to do the commandment and the law, which Moses the servant of the Lord charged you, to love the Lord your God, and to walk in all his ways, and to keep his commandments, and to cleave unto him, and to serve him with all your heart and with all your soul.

Psalms 1:2-3

But his delight is in the law of the Lord; and in his law doth he meditate day and night.

And he shall be like a tree planted by the rivers of water, that bringeth forth his fruit in his season; his leaf also shall not wither; and whatsoever he doeth shall prosper.

Psalms 51:6-7

Behold, thou desirest truth in the inward parts: and in the hidden part thou shalt make me to know wisdom.

Purge me with hyssop, and I shall be clean: wash me, and I shall be whiter than snow.

Isaiah 26:3

Thou wilt keep him in perfect peace, whose mind is stayed on thee: because he trusteth in thee.

Romans 8:6

For to be carnally minded is death; but to be spiritually minded is life and peace.

Romans 14:17

For the kingdom of God is not meat and drink; but righteousness, and peace, and joy in the Holy Ghost.

1 Corinthians 3:1-3

And I, brethren, could not speak unto you as unto spiritual, but as unto carnal, even as unto babes in Christ.

I have fed you with milk, and not with meat: for hitherto ye were not able to bear it, neither yet now are ye able.

For ye are yet carnal: for whereas there is among you envying, and strife, and divisions, are ye not carnal, and walk as men?

1 Corinthians 13:11

When I was a child, I spake as a child, I understood as a child, I thought as a child: but when I became a man, I put away childish things

1 Corinthians 14:20

Brethren, be not children in understanding: howbeit in malice be ye children, but in understanding be men.

Ephesians 4:13-15

Till we all come in the unity of the faith, and of the knowledge of the Son of God, unto a perfect man, unto the measure of the stature of the fulness of Christ:

That we henceforth be no more children, tossed to and fro, and carried about with every wind of doctrine, by the sleight of men, and cunning craftiness, whereby they lie in wait to deceive;

But speaking the truth in love, may grow up into him in all things, which is the head, even Christ.

Philippians 3:15

Let us therefore, as many as be perfect, be thus minded: and if in any thing ye be otherwise minded, God shall reveal even this unto you.

Colossians 3:1-3

If ye then be risen with Christ, seek those things which are above, where Christ sitteth on the right hand of God.

Set your affection on things above, not on things on the earth.

For ye are dead, and your life is hid with Christ in God.

Hebrews 5:13-14

For every one that useth milk is unskilful in the word of righteousness: for he is a babe.

But strong meat belongeth to them that are of full age, even those who by reason of use have their senses exercised to discern both good and evil.

41

STRENGTH

Although it should not, life will destroy us, unless we are strong enough to survive it. Those who are strong in the Lord are like a boxer who refuses to stay down. If something knocks him down, he bounces back. The strength of the Lord will help us overcome every obstacle, including stress, depression, and burnout.

Deuteronomy 33:25

Thy shoes shall be iron and brass; and as thy days, so shall thy strength be.

2 Samuel 22:40

For thou hast girded me with strength to battle: them that rose up against me hast thou subdued under me.

Nehemiah 8:10

Then he said unto them, Go your way, eat the fat, and drink the sweet, and send portions unto them for whom nothing is prepared: for this day is holy unto our Lord: neither be ye sorry; for the joy of the Lord is your strength.

Psalms 18:32

It is God that girdeth me with strength, and maketh my way perfect.

Psalms 27:14

Wait on the LORD: be of good courage, and he shall strengthen thine heart: wait, I say, on the LORD.

Psalms 29:11

The LORD will give strength unto his people; the LORD will bless his people with peace.

Psalms 119:28

My soul melteth for heaviness: strengthen thou me according unto thy word.

Psalms 138:3

In the day when I cried thou answeredst me, and strengthenedst me with strength in my soul.

Proverbs 10:29

The way of the LORD is strength to the upright: but destruction shall be to the workers of iniquity.

Proverbs 18:10

The name of the LORD is a strong tower: the righteous runneth into it, and is safe.

Isaiah 40:29-31

He giveth power to the faint; and to them that have no might he increaseth strength.

Even the youths shall faint and be weary, and the young men shall utterly fall:

But they that wait upon the LORD shall renew their strength; they shall mount up with wings as eagles;

they shall run, and not be weary; and they shall walk, and not faint.

Isaiah 41:10

Fear thou not; for I am with thee: be not dismayed; for I am thy God: I will strengthen thee; yea, I will help thee; yea, I will uphold thee with the right hand of my righteousness.

2 Corinthians 12:9

And he said unto me, My grace is sufficient for thee: for my strength is made perfect in weakness. Most gladly therefore will I rather glory in my infirmities, that the power of Christ may rest upon me.

Ephesians 3:16

That he would grant you, according to the riches of his glory, to be strengthened with might by his Spirit in the inner man

Philippians 4:13

I can do all things through Christ which strengtheneth me.

Colossians 1:11

Strengthened with all might, according to his glorious power, unto all patience and longsuffering with joyfulness.

Stress is
nothing more
than a socially
acceptable
form of mental
illness.

— Richard Carlson

42

STRESS

There is no such thing as "good stress." Stress is a major contributor to the top six medical causes of death. When faced with stress, our bodies generate certain chemicals to assist us in the process. However, if we do not remove that stress, those chemicals designed to protect us during stress, become killers. We must do what we must to remove stress from our lives.

Psalms 62:2-8

He [God] *only is my rock and my salvation; he is my defence; I shall not be greatly moved.*

How long will ye imagine mischief against a man? ye shall be slain all of you: as a bowing wall shall ye be, and as a tottering fence.

They only consult to cast him down from his excellency: they delight in lies: they bless with their mouth, but they curse inwardly. Selah.

My soul, wait thou only upon God; for my expectation is from him.

He only is my rock and my salvation: he is my defence; I shall not be moved.

In God is my salvation and my glory: the rock of my strength, and my refuge, is in God.

Trust in him at all times; ye people, pour out your heart before him: God is a refuge for us. Selah.

Proverbs 29:25

The fear of man bringeth a snare: but whoso putteth his trust in the LORD shall be safe.

Isaiah 40:30-31

Even the youths shall faint and be weary, and the young men shall utterly fall:

But they that wait upon the LORD shall renew their strength; they shall mount up with wings as eagles; they shall run, and not be weary; and they shall walk, and not faint.

Romans 8:31

What shall we then say to these things? If God be for us, who can be against us?

Romans 8:37-39

Nay, in all these things we are more than conquerors through him that loved us.

For I am persuaded, that neither death, nor life, nor angels, nor principalities, nor powers, nor things present, nor things to come,

Nor height, nor depth, nor any other creature, shall be able to separate us from the love of God, which is in Christ Jesus our Lord.

Philippians 4:6-7

Be careful for nothing; but in every thing by prayer and supplication with thanksgiving let your requests be made known unto God.

And the peace of God, which passeth all understanding, shall keep your hearts and minds through Christ Jesus.

43

SUBMISSION

Submission begins where agreement ends. It is impossible to be in submission to anyone unless there is disagreement – otherwise one is only agreeing. We have trouble many times because we are not willing to submit to God-ordained authority over our lives. We can save ourselves much heartache and stress when we learn to submit to each other, and those who have the rule over us.

Matthew 26:39

And he went a little further, and fell on his face, and prayed, saying, O my Father, if it be possible, let this cup pass from me: nevertheless not as I will, but as thou wilt.

Matthew 26:42

He went away again the second time, and prayed, saying, O my Father, if this cup may not pass away from me, except I drink it, thy will be done.

Luke 14:27

And whosoever doth not bear his cross, and come after me, cannot be my disciple.

Ephesians 5:21-25

Submitting yourselves one to another in the fear of God.

Wives, submit yourselves unto your own husbands, as unto the Lord.

For the husband is the head of the wife, even as Christ is the head of the church: and he is the saviour of the body.

Therefore as the church is subject unto Christ, so let the wives be to their own husbands in every thing.

Husbands, love your wives, even as Christ also loved the church, and gave himself for it.

Hebrews 5:8

Though he were a Son, yet learned he obedience by the things which he suffered.

Hebrews 13:7

Remember them which have the rule over you, who have spoken unto you the word of God: whose faith follow, considering the end of their conversation.

Hebrews 13:17

Obey them that have the rule over you, and submit yourselves: for they watch for your souls, as they that must give account, that they may do it with joy, and not with grief: for that is unprofitable for you.

James 4:7

Submit yourselves therefore to God. Resist the devil, and he will flee from you.

1 Peter 5:5

Likewise, ye younger, submit yourselves unto the elder. Yea, all of you be subject one to another, and be clothed with humility: for God resisteth the proud, and giveth grace to the humble.

44

SUCCESS

Success is not a destination – it is a journey. We often get frustrated on our journey when success does not happen as quickly as we think it should. When this happens, it brings stress into our lives. The virtue of patience will aid us on our success journey and help us remain less stressful.

Joshua 1:6-8

Be strong and of a good courage: for unto this people shalt thou divide for an inheritance the land, which I sware unto their fathers to give them.

Only be thou strong and very courageous, that thou mayest observe to do according to all the law, which Moses my servant commanded thee: turn not from it to the right hand or to the left, that thou mayest prosper whithersoever thou goest.

This book of the law shall not depart out of thy mouth; but thou shalt meditate therein day and night, that thou mayest observe to do according to all that is written therein: for then thou shalt make thy way prosperous, and then thou shalt have good success.

1 Kings 2:3

And keep the charge of the Lord thy God, to walk in his ways, to keep his statutes, and his commandments, and his judgments, and his testimonies, as it is written in the law of Moses, that thou mayest prosper in all that thou doest, and whithersoever thou turnest thyself

Psalms 1:3

And he shall be like a tree planted by the rivers of water, that bringeth forth his fruit in his season; his leaf also shall not wither; and whatsoever he doeth shall prosper.

1 Chronicles 22:11

Now, my son, the Lord be with thee; and prosper thou, and build the house of the Lord thy God, as he hath said of thee.

2 Chronicles 20:20

And they rose early in the morning, and went forth into the wilderness of Tekoa: and as they went forth, Jehoshaphat stood and said, Hear me, O Judah, and ye inhabitants of Jerusalem; Believe in the Lord your God, so shall ye be established; believe his prophets, so shall ye prosper.

Ecclesiastes 10:10

If the iron be blunt, and he do not whet the edge, then must he put to more strength: but wisdom is profitable to direct.

Ecclesiastes 11:6

In the morning sow thy seed, and in the evening withhold not thine hand: for thou knowest not whether shall prosper, either this or that, or whether they both shall be alike good.

Romans 1:10

Making request, if by any means now at length I might have a prosperous journey by the will of God to come unto you.

45

THOUGHT LIFE

In addition to our words, the way we think is probably one of the most important actions in our lives. We become what we think. People have died without a physical cause for the death – they continually thought they were sick until the thoughts became reality. If we think right, it will help us overcome stress, depression, and burnout.

Psalms 119:59

I thought on my ways, and turned my feet unto thy testimonies.

Proverbs 12:5

The thoughts of the righteous are right: but the counsels of the wicked are deceit.

Proverbs 15:28

The heart of the righteous studieth to answer: but the mouth of the wicked poureth out evil things.

Proverbs 21:5

The thoughts of the diligent tend only to plenteousness; but of every one that is hasty only to want.

Proverbs 23:7

For as he thinketh in his heart, so is he: Eat and drink, saith he to thee; but his heart is not with thee.

Romans 12:2

And be not conformed to this world: but be ye transformed by the renewing of your mind, that ye may prove what is that good, and acceptable, and perfect, will of God.

1 Corinthians 2:16

For who hath known the mind of the Lord, that he may instruct him? But we have the mind of Christ.

Ephesians 3:20

Now unto him that is able to do exceeding abundantly above all that we ask or think, according to the power that worketh in us,

Ephesians 4:23-24

And be renewed in the spirit of your mind;

And that ye put on the new man, which after God is created in righteousness and true holiness.

Philippians 4:7-8

And the peace of God, which passeth all understanding, shall keep your hearts and minds through Christ Jesus.

Finally, brethren, whatsoever things are true, whatsoever things are honest, whatsoever things are just, whatsoever things are pure, whatsoever things are lovely, whatsoever things are of good report; if there be any virtue, and if there be any praise, think on these things.

Colossians 3:2

Set your affection on things above, not on things on the earth.

46

TIME MANAGEMENT

We have eighty-six thousand, four hundred deposited into an account for us every day. We must spend all of them. We cannot save any and carry them over to another time. The account is life. The deposit is seconds. God gives us time. We trade that time for anything else we want or need. How we use the time has a direct bearing on our stress levels. We must manage our time well.

Psalms 32:6

For this shall every one that is godly pray unto thee in a time when thou mayest be found: surely in the floods of great waters they shall not come nigh unto him.

Psalms 39:5

Behold, thou hast made my days as an handbreadth; and mine age is as nothing before thee: verily every man at his best state is altogether vanity. Selah.

Psalms 69:13

But as for me, my prayer is unto thee, O Lord, in an acceptable time: O God, in the multitude of thy mercy hear me, in the truth of thy salvation.

Psalms 90:12

So teach us to number our days, that we may apply our hearts unto wisdom.

Psalms 144:4

Man is like to vanity: his days are as a shadow that passeth away.

Isaiah 49:8

Thus saith the Lord, In an acceptable time have I heard thee, and in a day of salvation have I helped thee: and I will preserve thee, and give thee for a covenant of the people, to establish the earth, to cause to inherit the desolate heritages

Romans 13:11-12

And that, knowing the time, that now it is high time to awake out of sleep: for now is our salvation nearer than when we believed.

The night is far spent, the day is at hand: let us therefore cast off the works of darkness, and let us put on the armour of light.

Ephesians 5:15-16

See then that ye walk circumspectly, not as fools, but as wise,

Redeeming the time, because the days are evil.

James 4:14

Whereas ye know not what shall be on the morrow. For what is your life? It is even a vapour, that appeareth for a little time, and then vanisheth away.

if I had not
tithed the first
dollar I made
I would not
have tithed the
first million
dollars I made.

—John D.
Rockefeller, Sr.

47

TITHING

This subject has become contentious among some. However, it is still Biblical. The tithe belongs to God. If we do not honor the principle of tithing, it places us in the category of "thief," in the eyes of God. This will add stress to our lives, because God withholds His blessings. When we give God what is His, He rebukes the things that hinder our blessings.

Genesis 14:20

And blessed be the most high God, which hath delivered thine enemies into thy hand. And he gave him tithes of all.

Exodus 22:29

Thou shalt not delay to offer the first of thy ripe fruits, and of thy liquors: the firstborn of thy sons shalt thou give unto me.

Deuteronomy 14:22

Thou shalt truly tithe all the increase of thy seed, that the field bringeth forth year by year.

Numbers 18:25-26

And the Lord spake unto Moses, saying,

Thus speak unto the Levites, and say unto them, When ye take of the children of Israel the tithes which I have given you from them for your inheritance, then ye shall offer up an heave offering of it for the Lord, even a tenth part of the tithe.

Proverbs 3:9-10

Honour the Lord with thy substance, and with the firstfruits of all thine increase:

So shall thy barns be filled with plenty, and thy presses shall burst out with new wine.

Malachi 3:8

Will a man rob God? Yet ye have robbed me. But ye say, Wherein have we robbed thee? In tithes and offerings.

Matthew 23:23

Woe unto you, scribes and Pharisees, hypocrites! for ye pay tithe of mint and anise and cummin, and have omitted the weightier matters of the law, judgment, mercy, and faith: these ought ye to have done, and not to leave the other undone.

1 Corinthians 6:10

Nor thieves, nor covetous, nor drunkards, nor revilers, nor extortioners, shall inherit the kingdom of God.

Hebrews 7:5-9

And verily they that are of the sons of Levi, who receive the office of the priesthood, have a commandment to take tithes of the people according to the law, that is, of their brethren, though they come out of the loins of Abraham:

But he whose descent is not counted from them received tithes of Abraham, and blessed him that had the promises.

And without all contradiction the less is blessed of the better.

And here men that die receive tithes; but there he receiveth them, of whom it is witnessed that he liveth.

And as I may so say, Levi also, who receiveth tithes, payed tithes in Abraham.

48

VICTORY

Very little feels better or helps our self-esteem than celebrating a victory in the battle of life. Victories have an ability to elevate people out of the doldrums and pressures they face every day. However, it is not enough to gain a victory; the individual must also take some time and properly celebrate it, before moving to the next challenge. God designed us to be winners regardless of what life may be throwing at us.

Psalms 20:5

We will rejoice in thy salvation, and in the name of our God we will set up our banners: the LORD fulfil all thy petitions.

Psalms 44:5

Through thee will we push down our enemies: through thy name will we tread them under that rise up against us.

Psalms 55:18

He hath delivered my soul in peace from the battle that was against me: for there were many with me.

Psalms 76:5-6

The stouthearted are spoiled, they have slept their sleep: and none of the men of might have found their hands.

At thy rebuke, O God of Jacob, both the chariot and horse are cast into a dead sleep.

Proverbs 11:14

Where no counsel is, the people fall: but in the multitude of counsellors there is safety.

Micah 7:8

Rejoice not against me, O mine enemy: when I fall, I shall arise; when I sit in darkness, the LORD shall be a light unto me.

Luke 10:19

Behold, I give unto you power to tread on serpents and scorpions, and over all the power of the enemy: and nothing shall by any means hurt you.

John 16:33

These things I have spoken unto you, that in me ye might have peace. In the world ye shall have tribulation: but be of good cheer; I have overcome the world.

Romans 8:37-39

Nay, in all these things we are more than conquerors through him that loved us.

For I am persuaded, that neither death, nor life, nor angels, nor principalities, nor powers, nor things present, nor things to come,

Nor height, nor depth, nor any other creature, shall be able to separate us from the love of God, which is in Christ Jesus our Lord.

2 Corinthians 2:14

Now thanks be unto God, which always causeth us to triumph in Christ, and maketh manifest the savour of his knowledge by us in every place.

1 John 4:4

Ye are of God, little children, and have overcome them: because greater is he that is in you, than he that is in the world.

49

WORK

This is a unique topical application. Unique in that it is necessary, but also if improperly planned, it may be the source of much stress. God demands that we work. However, we must insure that we work smart. If we allow God to direct our paths, our work may be hard, but it does not have to stress us, depress us, or burn us out.

Genesis 2:15

And the Lord God took the man, and put him into the garden of Eden to dress it and to keep it.

Exodus 34:21

Six days thou shalt work, but on the seventh day thou shalt rest: in earing time and in harvest thou shalt rest.

Proverbs 13:11

Wealth gotten by vanity shall be diminished: but he that gathereth by labour shall increase.

Proverbs 14:23

In all labour there is profit: but the talk of the lips tendeth only to penury.

Ecclesiastes 9:10

Whatsoever thy hand findeth to do, do it with thy might; for there is no work, nor device, nor knowledge, nor wisdom, in the grave, whither thou goest.

Jeremiah 22:13

Woe unto him that buildeth his house by unrighteousness, and his chambers by wrong; that useth his neighbour's service without wages, and giveth him not for his work.

Luke 10:7

And in the same house remain, eating and drinking such things as they give: for the labourer is worthy of his hire. Go not from house to house.

Ephesians 4:28

Let him that stole steal no more: but rather let him labour, working with his hands the thing which is good, that he may have to give to him that needeth.

1 Thessalonians 4:11-12

And that ye study to be quiet, and to do your own business, and to work with your own hands, as we commanded you;

That ye may walk honestly toward them that are without, and that ye may have lack of nothing.

2 Thessalonians 3:10-13

For even when we were with you, this we commanded you, that if any would not work, neither should he eat.

For we hear that there are some which walk among you disorderly, working not at all, but are busybodies.

Now them that are such we command and exhort by our Lord Jesus Christ, that with quietness they work, and eat their own bread.

But ye, brethren, be not weary in well doing.

1 Timothy 5:18

For the scripture saith, Thou shalt not muzzle the ox that treadeth out the corn. And, The labourer is worthy of his reward.

50

WORSHIP

Worship directs our attention away from ourselves, and our problems, and focuses it upon God. Worship is the means whereby we pass beyond the veil and into the Holy of Holies of the Lord God Almighty. Getting into His glory is the key to eradicating the stress in our lives.

1 Chronicles 16:29

Give unto the Lord the glory due unto his name: bring an offering, and come before him: worship the Lord in the beauty of holiness.

Psalms 5:7

But as for me, I will come into thy house in the multitude of thy mercy: and in thy fear will I worship toward thy holy temple.

Psalms 29:1-2

Give unto the Lord, O ye mighty, give unto the Lord glory and strength.

Give unto the Lord the glory due unto his name; worship the Lord in the beauty of holiness.

Psalms 95:6

O come, let us worship and bow down: let us kneel before the Lord our maker.

Psalms 96:9

O worship the Lord in the beauty of holiness: fear before him, all the earth.

Psalms 99:5

Exalt ye the Lord our God, and worship at his footstool; for he is holy.

Matthew 4:10

Then saith Jesus unto him, Get thee hence, Satan: for it is written, Thou shalt worship the Lord thy God, and him only shalt thou serve.

John 4:24

God is a Spirit: and they that worship him must worship him in spirit and in truth.

Hebrews 12:28-29

Wherefore we receiving a kingdom which cannot be moved, let us have grace, whereby we may serve God acceptably with reverence and godly fear:

For our God is a consuming fire.

James 4:8

Draw nigh to God, and he will draw nigh to you. Cleanse your hands, ye sinners; and purify your hearts, ye double minded.